The Herb Lady's Notebook

by
Venus Catherine Andrecht

The Herb Lady's Notebook

by
Venus Catherine Andrecht

Photography — Joe Butts
Calligraphy — Margaret L. McWhorter
Illustrations — Venus C. Andrecht

Ransom Hill Press
P.O. Box 325
Ramona, California
92065

© 1992 Venus Andrecht, 11th Edition

Printed in the United states of America

ISBN 0-9604342-4-0

Library of Congress Catalog Number   83-63072

DEDICATION

Dedicated to all my formerly sick friends and desperate strangers. If you hadn't been ignorant enough to let me practice on you, my life would never have become devoted to bowel movements, tape worm sizes, bald heads and billiousness.

Thanks so very much for expanding my interests.

NOTICE

The author does not prescribe herbs, nor directly, or indirectly, dispense medical advice. This book was written to inform and educate people regarding the historical and traditional uses of herbs. Nutritionists, herbalists and other experts in the field of health and nutrition hold widely varying views. It is not the intent of the author to prescribe or diagnose. It is the intent to offer health information that will assist you in cooperating with your doctor in the mutual problem of building and maintaining your health. If you use this information without your doctor's approval, you are prescribing for yourself, which is your right, but the author and publisher assume no responsibility.

FOREWORD

Venus said, "Judy, I was going to have a famous person write my foreword. Then I thought, 'No. What I really need is an **ordinary** person. Someone like everyone else. Judy would be perfect.'"

So, here I am, folks. Your regular, garden-variety woman with a common story: I used to get up three hours earlier in the morning than I should have. Why? Because I had to make sure I could go to the bathroom before I left for work.

I'd comb my hair. Then trot to the bathroom. No luck. Put on my make-up. Off to the bathroom. No luck. Drink three cups of coffee. Off to the bathroom. I generally got in two hours of frenzied sitting before I left for work. Then I met Venus.

"You're a fool," she said. "What are you doing up at 4 a.m.? A toilet seat is too cold at that hour."

I agreed and sceptically put myself on an herb program. A month later, the sun began getting up before I did.

After six months, I found The Old Judy had passed away. Gone were most of my depressions, testy temperment, crummy headaches and sneaky gas. After eight months the cellulite began melting off my thighs. One day I tried on the jeans I had when I married. They fit!

I found I slept better, felt better and ate less.

Today, I continue to take herbs. Not only **take** them, but teach classes and help **other** people take herbs.

What can I say? They changed my life. They can change yours.

Signed,

Judy Bachofer

ORDINARY JUDY BACHOFER

v.

ACKNOWLEDGEMENT

Many herb uses and programs are like myths. They've been passed by word of mouth for so long that I haven't a clue as to who put what together. I've given credit where I can, but apologize for leaving out others.

I'd like to publicly thank my daughter, Summer, for allowing me to leave in her story under *"Terrible Adolescence."* When she read it, she screamed, "I'm ruined! All my friends will read this!" Her compassion prevailed. She was finally convinced that her story might help many children her age.

I also want to thank my father, Jim McWhorter, for allowing me to expose his foibles to the nation.

Thanks to Ludmilla and Isaac, my adventurous and innovative friends from Montana.

And, of course, thanks to Helen Duval of *"Hairball"* and *"Cat Scratch"* fame. It would have been a dull book without the five of you.

Table Of Contents

INTRODUCTION

You're likely to become quite annoyed with me when you keep running into, for example:

Combination B-10
Capsicum
Ginseng
Gotu Kola

OR

Combination B-15
Valerian Root
Skullcap Herb
Hops Flowers

You may say, "Heck fire! Why can't the woman just give the name of that fool combination so I can rush to the store and buy it?"

I'd love to do that. I'd like to make it easy for you. However, legally, I can't. Also, there are too many herb companies with similar combinations, and all have different names for their combinations. So...You have to be a detective.

It certainly is easier to buy the formulas already made up than to try to mix your own. So take this book to the health food store and check the herb combinations against different herb bottles. You're going to find some of them and others that are close enough.

Look through various health magazines for ads from herb companies. Write and ask for information. Some of the best herb companies sell through distributors or mail order. You'll have to work for your good health, but it will be more than worth your effort.

You'll notice the words "historically" and "traditionally" liberally scattered throughout this book. There's a reason for this. I can't legally diagnose or prescribe. If I did, you'd be bringing me picnic baskets...in jail. But, "historically" said, is OK. "Historically" means dead people said it and dead people have credibility. "Traditionally" is also a safe word to use because it means everyone has always said it down through the ages. Anything said that many years has got to be true, right?

Also, to protect myself, with this book, I function as a reporter. I report what I have done, or would do, and what other people are doing, or have done. All reports are true and come from my files. Only the names are changed to protect the indignant.

PART I

Why Take Herbs

"...When a man loses his health, then he first begins to take care of it..."

Josh Billings

Helen's Hairball

My office door flew open. With a dramatic flourish Helen announced, "Venus, I passed a hairball last night!" She whipped a glass bottle from her purse and plunked it on my desk. I sat uneasily and eyed the bottle. Helen stood proud. A pleased grin broke out on her face. As my right hand lady in the shop, Helen was pretty sure she knew what would delight me. Her short grayish curls danced. Nodding her head she continued, "I used to chew my hair in grammar school. I was real nervous, so I'd pull my hair around and chew on it all day. That was sixty years ago." She pointed proudly at the thing in the bottle, "That's a hairball." She gave a shudder. "I passed it this morning in my bowel movement. Pretty good, huh?" She looked at me, her thin body tense with expectation. She waited for my approval.

"Great," I said. "That's wonderful, Helen."

Helen sat down across from me and clasped her hands on my desk. "I did good, huh?" Her loop-earrings with-the-stars bounced and swung. "I figured you'd be happy with the hairball for your collection."

I slowly picked up Helen's specimen. I noted the pieces of tapeworm floating in alcohol, some nameless bits of something and the so-called hairball. Strange. I stood up and carried the bottle to the front door where the light was better. Heck, I needed to be outside for this one. Helen trailed behind me. I held the glass to the morning sun. I turned it around and around again. Looked under it...Helen hung over my shoulder chattering about the old school days sixty years ago and wasn't it a scream that after all these years a darn hairball would come out!

Suddenly I yelled, "Hey, look at that! This guy's got **lips**! My gosh! Look at that body! Helen, look at that body!" I juggled the bottle so the pink creature jounced. Its spikes cut through the water. It had lips all right. Big fat ones. "Helen, look at those lips!" I turned around. No Helen. "Come here, Helen." I pleaded, "You've got to see this guy. Boy, you passed a good one."

I studied the fleshy creature more closely, my eyes squinting against the sun. It was about the size of a nickel. What Helen had thought was hair appeared to be made of stronger stuff; like hairy spikes. It made my skin crawl in a real fun way. After all, I hadn't passed it.

"Come on, Helen," I cried enthusiastically. "Where are you?" Getting no response I turned and trotted back to my herb room. There was Helen lying flat on the couch.

"Oh gosh," I said. I sat beside her. She was pale. "I'm sorry," I ventured. "Maybe it's a hairball, Helen. I could be wrong."

Helen was silent. She stared at me blankly. "Yep," I soothed, "It's probably a hairball. It does look like a lot of hair there." I patted her hand. "Sure, that's what it is, a hairball. It happens all the time."

Helen stirred and looked hopeful. "You think so?" she asked.

"Oh yes," I answered. "That's it all right." I looked at her brightly and said, "And anyway, better **out** than **in**, right Helen?"

"Yes, I suppose so," she agreed.

"Tell you what," I said, "Why don't you just rest here a bit while I put some stock away." I gave her head a little rub and got up. "I'm sure it's just a lousy hairball."

"But, I'll tell you what," I muttered quietly as I moved toward my shelves, "I never saw a hairball with lips."

The Bowel

Helen was the willing victim of an herbal cleanse. One of the gigantic, whopper **clean-out-the-crud** cleanses. She had embarked on the cleanse willingly because she understood a few basic health facts. Almost every naturopath and herbalist will tell you that:

90% of all disease comes from the bowel.[1]

90% of all symptoms come from the bowel.

90% of all people have worms.

Helen also knew that when people eat the good old American diet (white flour, white sugar, canned goods, boxed goods, etc.) a lot of it passes through and a lot of it doesn't. Processed foods have a tendency to stick to the walls of the intestine, and stay there. One reformed junk food lady I know likes to tell people how she ate as a kid.

"I used to have a 'Twinkie Bowel.' That's the kind of stuff I ate. My mom did her best by us. She thought a dinner of hot dogs, canned vegetables, jello and white bread was a meal put together by a **good mother**. I'd sit there at the table and take the white bread and chew it up. Then when it got gummy I'd roll it into a ball and smash and stick it to the roof of my mouth. Then I'd see how much I could eat and swallow before the white bread would fall off the top of my mouth. Sometimes I could get through a whole meal."

Can you imagine what happens to your bowel when you've been eating this way all your life? I've read that when autopsies are done on people, the coroners find anywhere from ten to sixty pounds of this old, dried fecal material packed in and lining the bowel. You wonder why you have a potbelly?

The next time you see a man lumbering down the street with his little

1. *Childhood Diseases*, Dr. John R. Christopher

average bowel

sweater barely covering a beachball stomach, you can think to yourself, "That guy's not fat. He's just full of old poopy."

There's a lot of old fecal material in the bowel and much of it has been there for years and years. In a sense, it becomes layered, year by year. As this happens, weaker areas may tend to balloon out forming large or small pockets where more old fecal material becomes lodged. Now you've got all this rotten debris resting in your bowel. Only it's not just resting. It's toxic and a lot of it is being absorbed into the body, or by specific organs.

This is why health practitioners say that 90 percent of all disease and symptoms come from the bowel. And the worms? What does nature do when something is decaying and rotting? She sends in creatures to clean it up. So you may have more close friends than your address book shows.

You may find all of this startling, shocking, crude or unbelievable. Wait until you try a good herbal cleanse! You may still find it startling, shocking, crude and unbelievable, but the evidence will be right there before you.

I've had many people who are on a cleanse call me up. "Venus! I can't believe this! Tons of old stuff is coming out! But where is it coming from? I haven't been eating nearly that much. How can all that possibly be inside me?"

I had one lucky lady talk to me after she had, of her own volition, put herself on a watermelon-only diet for three months. She told me that for more than a month and one half, she had normal bowel movements. Just like she was still eating. It took another month and a half before she was passing only straight watermelon. Isn't that unbelievable?

Another woman simply began taking *Cascara Sagrada* and called me one morning at six. She couldn't wait until I'd gotten up because she was too excited. "I had a bowel movement just now at least twenty inches long!"

These cleanses do get very exciting. It's nice to have the whole family, or your friends, take them with you. It brings friends and families closer. You find a common bond.

"Hey, Marian, what'd you pass today?"

"Boy, Denise, you won't believe this..."

"Oh, hey, I can top that one. You should see what I've got in a bottle."

"Say, you remember that toothbrush I lost three years ago?"

One marine got his whole platoon talked into a bowel cleanse. "Now," he says, "All the men do is sit on the pot and socialize."

4

Cleanses
Comfrey-Pepsin Cleanse

What I've been working up to is one of my favorite cleanses. Many people take this when their lives get dull. Or they feel fat. Or under par. It's a good **starter cleanse** for people who've never tried herbs because what you **see** is usually what you can **believe** and I always see results with this one. I call it the *Comfrey-Pepsin Cleanse*. It was given to me by an herbalist in Arizona. She said a number of people had used it with many benefits. She found that fat people lost weight and thin ones gained. She told me electrifying stories of regained health and interesting side effects. One of **her** side effects was the most intriguing. But before we get to that let me explain the cleanse.

This cleanse is designed to work on the entire digestive system. This includes the mouth, esophagus, stomach, small intestine and large intestine. Many people don't realize it, but they have a thick mucus coating the length of their digestive track. This mucus gets hard like glass or plastic. It becomes difficult for the person to absorb their nutrients, including herbs and vitamins. Many fat people eat so much because they're actually starving. They aren't absorbing what the body needs. The *Comfrey-Pepsin Cleanse* is designed to dissolve and release this mucus. Along with pushing out old fecal material from various bowel pockets, it purges free-loaders (parasites).

Fat people tend to lose weight on this cleanse. Skinny ones gain.

Carol's Comfrey-Pepsin Cleanse

1. If I were **constipated** (less than two bowel movements a day), I'd take:

> One or two *Enzyme* or *Hydrochloric Acid* tablets per meal. Two *Comfrey* with *Pepsin* capsules **after** every meal, **opened** into a beverage of some kind.
>
> A **Bowel Cleansing Combination**[2] of my choice. I would take enough to get three bowel movements a day. If I remained plugged up I would take added *Cascara Sagrada* and perhaps some enemas.
>
> This would be balanced out with two or three **Building Combinations**.

2. If I had **looser bowels** (two or three movements a day, naturally) or a **sensitive** or **irritable** bowel, I'd change the program a bit:

2. For information on combinations see Appendix I

5

One or two *Enzyme* or *Hydrochloric Acid* tablets with each meal.

One or two tablespoons of *Aloe Vera Juice* before meals.

Two *Comfrey* with *Pepsin* capsules **after** each meal **opened** into juice or water.

Two after each meal to calm the bowel:

> **Combination B-27**
> Comfrey Root
> Marshmallow Root
> Slippery Elm Bark
> Ginger Root
> Wild Yam Root
> Lobelia Herb

Enough of a **Bowel Cleansing Combination** to have three movements a day.

Plus two or three **Building Herbs** or **Combinations**. With a touchy colon I'd add *Slippery Elm* and *Psyllium Hulls*. It can help.

I make sure to **open** the capsules and take them **after** each meal. If they are swallowed, they often come straight through. On the cleanse you may pass things that look like capsules. They may be, if your digestion is poor. Or, they may be old fecal material (plugs) from pockets in the bowel. Here's a simple test. Fish out the suspicious items and dry them on a paper towel. Then cut them in half. What do they look like and how do they smell? If they smell totally terrible, I'd suspect they were plugs.

Most people take this cleanse until they've had two weeks free of mucus and parasites. But remember, the average bowel takes at least a year to cleanse.

Here are symptoms that various people have reported while on this cleanse:

"I feel better than I ever have in my life!"

"I'm passing all kinds of strange mucus shapes."

"I'm so dizzy I can't stand up."

"I feel nauseous."

"I don't want to eat anything but fruits, vegetables and juices. I can't stand the thought of junk food."

"Yesterday I passed hundreds of little black spiders."

"I passed a little black toad," or "A long red worm," or "Scores of fuzzy little balls with legs."

One skinny girl passed a long tapeworm and instantly lost her craving for sugar and a week later gained five pounds. One man had life-long bad breath. The kind where you walk into a room and know he's there. He'd tried everything. One week into the cleanse and you couldn't find him in the dark. He's delighted. And so are the rest of us! He's had sinus trouble for years. We think all those years of heavy drip gave him quite a layer of rotting mucus. Simple bowel cleanses and digesters hadn't touched his problem.

Another woman was continually surprised by unusual items. "A chunk of something with a plum seed in it. A thing shaped like a heart and a small roll of 'waxed paper.' Plugs that look like hooks and horns and a one by three inch balloon."

Of course people report the usual assortment of tapeworms, small worms, no worms, mucus, spaghetti-like stuff, and "bunches of alfalfa sprouts, only I don't eat alfalfa sprouts." And things that lead people screaming to their telephones to alert and alarm their relatives.

The Family That Cleans Together Cleaves Together

Let me tell you Carol's story. She's the Arizona herbalist that gave me the *Comfrey-Pepsin Cleanse*. Like any good herb lady, or man, would, she decided to try the new cleanse on **herself** before foisting it on her friends. She took the herbs faithfully for some weeks, being careful to **open** the *Comfrey-Pepsin* and take it **after** her meals. She took enough of the bowel cleansers to make sure she had a bowel movement at least three times a day. Now, my friends, when you're taking herbs, especially cleansing herbs, it's just natural, after you've had a bowel movement to turn around and look. If you're going to all that work, you want to know what you've accomplished. Right? With Carol, one day, the same as any other day, she turned around and looked; then she screamed and fell back against the sink.

"Oh! Oh help!" she yelled. "I've passed a jelly fish!"

There in the toilet was a pale creature with a hump for a body. It slid silently across the water. Carol lifted her head toward the ceiling and howled. Her husband and children came thundering up the stairs. They threw open the bathroom door. The jelly fish skittered across the water and dove to the bottom of the bowl. They screamed. Carol continued to scream. Most people can't continue hysteria forever, so eventually they calmed down and took a closer look.

Carol's brave husband fished out the jelly fish. They were puzzled to find that it was not a creature, but a large squarish piece of paper-like material. Apparently, as it slipped out of Carol, an air bubble had caught under the paper giving it its movement and shape. When the bubble popped, the "jelly fish" collapsed to the bottom of the bowl. How exciting! Now you can see how herbs bring families together. That little group talked for weeks.

Marvelous things come out in a cleanse. One lady keeps a big stick by her toilet...another a large silver spoon.

"That Helen Again"

On any cleanse use common sense. Helen (of hairball fame) called one day.

"Venus? I don't know what's the matter with me."

"Speak up Helen," I urged. "You sound so faint. I can hardly hear you."

"That's it," she said. "I feel so weak...so weak."

"Why?" I questioned. "What have you been doing? You're on the *Comfrey-Pepsin Cleanse* aren't you?...ah, oh..." A thought struck me. "Just how many times a day are you going to the bathroom?"

With a tired little voice Helen answered. "Fifteen."

Fifteen! We can get carried away here. With fifteen all your nutrients are washing right through you. Three or four bowel movements a day are plenty! Most natural healers say one after each meal is ideal.

Daddy Dearest

This story concerns my father. He's about sixty-five years old and loves his doctors. He specializes in heart trouble and depressions. He regularly takes to his bed with flus and nameless diseases that knock the nails out from under him. He's spent his life complaining about his health and being sick. He likes to moan and carry on. But, remarkably, you look at him and he's got this chubby-cheeked little face with no wrinkles and a full head of curly blond hair that grows up to a point. He hops around like a smooth-faced elf, watering his flowers and complaining. For several years after I found herbs I worked him over pretty good.

"Oh come on, Daddy. Try this one. *Hawthorn* is historically the best herb for the heart. I know it'll fix your problem."

"No," he'd say. "I'm taking enough stuff now, can't take any more."

"Oh come on, Dad! You're taking drugs. You can fit in one or two herbs."

"Nope!"

Then he'd go into a long harangue about how herbs wouldn't help him. But I'd keep trying. Every Christmas, birthday or visit I'd take him some new herb or combination that I was sure would fix him right up. Finally I said, "To heck with him! No matter what he does he'll live till he's ninety." I quit trying to help.

So I got a big surprise one day, a year or two later. I was having lunch with my parents and several sisters and brothers. I'd just discovered the *Comfrey-Pepsin Cleanse* and was explaining it in detail to them, but, pointedly ignoring my father. I raved about the symptoms, the herbs and the exciting results. I went on and on growing more enthusiastic and graphic. Mucus! Worms! Plugs! Weight loss! Harrowing, but fun, experiences!

My father spoke up, "I want to try that cleanse."

"What?" I hollered. "You? No way!" I went back to my descriptions.

Dad grabbed my arm. "I mean it. I want to take that cleanse."

"Oh come on, Daddy," I said. "You won't even take one herb and you want to take one like this?" I was incredulous. I refused. I wouldn't supply him. No way!

"Come on," Daddy begged. "Please, I mean it. I want to clean out my body."

I exchanged looks with the rest of my family. "Dad," I said. "You really think you can do something like this? I mean, I've tried for years..."

Mom spoke up laughing, "Oh, let him do it."

"Well, OK." I agreed. "But I sure can't believe this."

Dad had to have those herbs right away. I gave him the pile with careful and explicit instructions. "Dad, you're so full of drugs and poop and poisons that this may hit you hard. You do understand that you may have a lot of symptoms from this cleanse, don't you? It won't hurt you, but you may feel stinko."

"I'll be fine," he said. He snatched up his booty and trotted off. I felt nervous but let it pass.

Several days later my mother called. "Honey," she whispered into the phone, "don't ever give your father herbs again." My stomach dropped. Mom continued "He's laid out in bed. He says you've tried to kill him."

"What?" I shrieked. "He **begged** me for those herbs."

"I know," Mom soothed. "But you know your father..." She paused, then said reasonably, "Your father and his toxins are perfectly balanced...it's best not to disturb either one. Just leave them alone."

You don't need an exotic cleanse to see results.

My Simple Cleanse

I'd choose one of the following combinations:

Combination C-5		**Combination C-6**		**Combination C-7**
Pumpkin Seeds		Cascara Sagrada Bark		Cascara Sagrada Bark
Culver's Root		Buckthorn Bark		Rhubarb Root
Mandrake Root		Licorice Root		Golden Seal Root
Violet Leaves	OR	Capsicum Fruit	OR	Capsicum Fruit
Comfrey Root		Ginger Root		Ginger Root
Cascara Sagrada Bark		Barberry Rootbark		Barberry Rootbark
Witch Hazel Bark		Couch-grass Herb		Lobelia Herb
Mullein Leaves		Red Clover Tops		Fennel Seeds
Slippery Elm Bark		Lobelia Herb		Red Raspberry Leaves

9

These combinations are available in capsule form which makes taking them much easier.

If more action is needed I add straight *Cascara Sagrada*. (Just remember that *Cascara Sagrada* gives a very moving experience. It's called Sacred Bark by the Indians. I think it will leave you in awe, too.)

If diarrhea occurs with this I add *Psyllium Seed* or *Psyllium Hulls*. This is a plant that acts as a bulking agent and absorbs liquids. It swells up and tunnels through the body like a roto-rooter, pulling out pockets of old material that are lodged in the intestine. I stir a heaping teaspoon into a **full** glass of juice or water several times a day.

There are other herbs people add if they still aren't moving. One is *Cayenne Pepper* (or *Capsicum*). This stimulates the bowel to do its own work. Many people have taken a little too much *Cayenne Pepper*. When I first began taking herbs I took about eight capsules to get my circulation and bowels moving at a fast clip. Let me tell you, I was up at midnight with the hottest bottom in town. I kept dancing and moaning. I know for sure the feeling passes and leaves only a warm memory.

Alfalfa has been used by many people to traditionally add bulk to the bowel and trace elements and vitamins to the body.

Some people switch *Buckthorn* back and forth with *Cascara Sagrada*. *Buckthorn* is, historically, used as a laxative and for warts.

When I take a cleanse, as I mentioned, I usually add a bulking agent like *Psyllium* to prevent diarrhea.

When you first start you just never know how your body will react to bowel cleansers. "Better **out** than **in**" yes, but "Better **safe** than **sorry**." For example:

One lady I know, insisted that she wanted two bowel cleansers. Nothing else. She was quite emphatic about it. No builders.[3] No bulkers. She'd been constipated for years and knew she could handle these two.

It doesn't always pay to think you know it all. This lady took her two major movers and lost a load on the escalator at Sears.

I thought, "Wow! That's the last we, or the herbs, will ever see of her."

I was wrong. This lady was delighted. Now she knew for a fact that herbs really worked!

Many herbalists throw in a good blood cleanser with a bowel cleanser.

I choose from the following *Blood Cleansing Combinations*.

3. See Appendix I

Combination C-1	OR	OR
Yellow Dock Root		
Dandelion Root	**Combination C-2**	**Combination C-3**
Burdock Root	Red Clover Tops	Cascara Sagrada Bark
Licorice Root	Chaparral	Oregon Grape Root
Chaparral Herb	A Secret Herb[4]	Chaparral Herb
Red Clover Tops		Burdock Root
Barberry Rootbark		Buckthorn Bark
Cascara Sagrada Bark		Prickly Ash Bark
Yarrow Herb		Peach Bark
Sarsaparilla Root		Stillingia Root

OR

Single herbs: *Yellow Dock* or *Burdock*.

And **very important!** When doing a cleanse of any kind, most people take several builders. These give you strength. Otherwise, with all the cleansing, a person can feel very weak.

Startling Development

Fascinating but true. A young woman given to wearing short shorts went on a vacation. She didn't have a bowel movement for seven days. After she returned home she called me. She was frantic.

"I've got tons of boils on my rear end! One boil is so big, I've developed a pointed butt on one side! You should see me in shorts!"

Desperate, she took several bowel and blood cleansers. I'm happy to say, after a (short) while, her shorts fit again.

This is a Test

Do you want to know how quickly your body moves old fecal material out of the bowel? A chiropractor gave me this recipe: He has people drink:

Two tablespoons of straight (undiluted) *Liquid Chlorophyll.*

Note the time. Keep a sharp look out. The *Chlorophyll* should come out in the bowel movement in 12 to 48 hours. Some people who think things are moving along fine are horrified to see the green two weeks later.

---

4. Various herb companies have this formula, but will not reveal the secret herb

Sneaky Cleanse

Liquid cleanse products are available. When swallowed the liquid cleanse,(*Bentonite,* a clay) pulls poisons and toxins from the body. However, it also pulls out vitamins and minerals. I'd never take it for more than a week at a time or while I was pregnant.

I know a man named Adam who's pretty pure most of the time. However, whenever he does eat sugar or take a nip of liquor, he always follows his binge with a tablespoon of *Bentonite*. He figures it pulls his momentary lapse right through his body and out the back door.

Diane and Al's Clean Start Recipe

To one sixteen ounce glass add:
    One tablespoon *Psyllium Hulls*
    One tablespoon *Powdered Vitamin C*
    One third cup *Pure Water*
    Applejuice
Stir quickly, (or use a blender.)

Ivy's Sweep Out

    Two tablespoons *Aloe Vera Juice*
    Two tablespoons *Liquid Chlorophyll*
    One teaspoon *Psyllium Hulls*
    Two *Cascara Sagrada capsules*

Mix first three items in half a glass of apple juice, or juice of your choice. Drink immediately. Swallow the *Cascara Sagrada* with a full glass of water.

Interesting Sidelights

Blow Away Your Friends

An interesting side light of a beginning cleanse can be gas. The bowel isn't used to being joggled and worked on by aggressive herbal cleanses.

You've decided you don't want to amuse people with the orchestra in your innards? Some people use *Ginger*. It's been used by gassy folk for centuries.

Gas can also be caused by faulty digestion. When my father is feeling depressed he likes to remind me about the time he went shopping with my mother. They went to a women's clothing store. While Mom was trying on clothes Daddy waited impatiently.

"I was just standing by one of those circle things where the clothes all hang around it, you know? There were a couple of good looking women going through the dresses. Well, I was just standing there looking handsome, like I can do, when suddenly...you know, Venus," he said and looked real sheepish. "I let out this great big ripper, so bad it blew the clothes on the turnstile!" He gives me another sad, embarrassed-elf look, "Those ladies...those ladies hunched over and laughed at me and trotted off!"

I could save him from traumas like that with a little *Ginger*.

Now that you understand the basics of bowel cleansing, you might like this story.

An herbalist told me this older man came to see her as a new client. She sat him down and carefully explained how 90 percent of all problems and symptoms come from the bowel. That 90 percent of all people need to clean that area as it's preventing absorption and seeping toxins into the body. She explained that he was part of that 90 percent. He needed to clean his digestive tract. He looked at her thoughtfully.

"No," he said slowly, "I don't think so. My absorption is real good. I absorb everything I eat. I know that for a fact...very little ever comes out."

Worms

Even Ladies of Class Pass Gas

Once I gave a lecture in a ritzy home in a ritzy city. Tucked neatly into a large family room were a group of tastefully decorated ladies. As I looked across the troupe of women I saw soft beige suits, silky dresses, multiple strings of real pearls and soft leather shoes. A regular sea of money and class. Undaunted, I sped into my regular talk about the digestive system, working hard to elicit a few audience responses. There were none. Drawing a picture of the average bowel on the chalkboard brought forth no amazed exclamations. I mentioned several nurses I knew who had been present at bowel operations where doctors had to use hacksaws.

There were no startled tongue clickings from my group. I pulled out the heavy stuff.

"Well," I began, "A nurse told me this. She was present at a gallbladder operation. Upon opening the patient the doctor was startled.

'Hey, look at this one!' The gallbladder was packed with worms. They cleaned out all the worms then proceeded to clip out the healthy gallbladder.

'After all,' said the nurse, 'It **was** a gallbladder operation.' "

There were several titters and that was it. I tried a few more alarming tales. Nothing... I paused and gave the ladies my good exasperated look. They just sat there. Poised. Calm. At peace. Suddenly it struck me. There was no audience participation or concern because these ladies didn't have worms. Not a one of them. They knew they were too rich. Too clean. They didn't mingle with the rest of us. My head sagged a little. I realized that as far as they were concerned, they were just watching a good show with a rather crude entertainer. I looked over at the hostess. She smiled pleasantly.

Then, "Ladies!" From the front row a woman jumped up. She too was in soft beige with a string of lustrous pearls. Her short blonde hair shone with Miss Clairol's Instant Radiance. She raised her arms to the audience—"Girl's! Venus is telling you the truth. I know it for a fact!"

The group stirred. "I used to think, no way can I have worms. No way! But then" she lowered her voice, "I went to a health clinic. I started taking colonics..." The ladies looked puzzled. "You know," she said, "Where they flush your intestines with water and all kinds of things come out!"

Chairs squeaked as women squirmed..."And," she continued, "I took a full herbal program to kill parasites." She turned and pointed at me, "Venus is right! You should have seen the stuff that came out of me. Fat worms. Bunches of worms. And..." she emphasized, "all kinds of famous people went to this clinic. Movie stars. And politicians. And...well, you know, top people...and they passed worms too. I saw them!"

My audience came alive. "Thank you very much!" I said to my new friend. "Shall we go on?"

More Astounding Stories

Regarding worms, an herbalist told me this story and swears it's true. A lady she knew, who was going through a cleanse, was watching television with her husband one night. The woman sat there, calmly, knitting a toaster cover. Her husband glanced her way, turned back and glanced again. "Darling," he said hesitantly. "What's that hanging off your nose?" On closer inspection they found a few more things in her ears and eyes. Worms.[5]

Another woman had her ten-year-old daughter dewormed three times by the doctor. Each time she washed all the bedding. She washed all her clothes. Still the girl's pinworms returned. In due course, the rest of the family got "Wendy's worms" too. In desperation and because Wormy Wendy was developing a complex, her mother gave her powdered *Black Walnut Hulls*. That was the end of the pinworms. Normal family life resumed.

An interesting idea...worms and parasites are suspected as associates in various diseases like: Cancer. Lupus. Sinus trouble. Arthritis. Rheumatic Fever. Gallbladder and Prostate problems, etc.

Sinus Parasites

Remember the lady with the worm hanging off her nose? For anything suspicious in that area I'd use this for a while:

I'd take six capsules daily.

Combination C-11
Golden Seal Root
Black Walnut Hulls
Marshmallow Root
Lobelia Herb
Plantain Herb
Bugleweed Herb

PLUS
I'd take six capsules daily.
Combination B-28
Golden Seal Root
Capsicum Fruit
Myrrh Gum

AND
I'd take six capsules daily: *Black Walnut.*

Historic Worm Evictors
Chaparral
Black Walnut Hulls
Garlic

---

5. *Parasites We Humans Harbor*, Aaron E. Klein

Plain and Simple

To any regular herb program or cleanse, I often add one of the historic worm evictors.

For example: I take, *Black Walnut Hulls,* four capsules a day, four bottles worth.

Utah Worm Getter

This worm program comes from a lady in Utah who used it successfully on herself. The first day she took four capsules of this combination:

Combination C-5
Pumpkin Seeds
Culver's Root
Mandrake Root
Violet Leaves
Comfrey Root
Cascara Sagrada Bark
Witch Hazel Bark
Mullein Leaves
Slippery Elm Bark

The second day she took:

Four capsules of *Garlic* and four capsules of *Black Walnut Hulls.*

She alternated **Combination C-5** with the four capsules each of *Garlic* and *Black Walnut Hulls* over a period of three weeks.

Digestion

Cleansing the bowel is so interesting that little is said about **digestion**. When a person has a physical problem the great temptation is to jump right in and work the heck out of that ailment, much like a specialist who focuses exclusively on the heart, kidneys, toes or whatever, to the exclusion of the patient. But the person with a particular body malfunction must recognize something. If their digestion is poor, they won't absorb any of the nutritive food elements that herbs supply.

If a person is ill, more than likely, their digestion **is** off. Why spend a paycheck on herbs and vitamins and feed them to the toilet several days later? If I had poor digestion I'd probably start with the *Comfrey-Pepsin Cleanse*, since it covers all bases, but here are a few other ideas:

Better Digestion Herbally

Historically used for gas and heartburn.

Combination B-24

Papaya Fruit	Fennel Seeds
Ginger Root	Lobelia Herb
Peppermint Leaves	Spearmint Leaves
Wild Yam Root	Catnip Herb

I'd take two to three each meal.

Papaya and *Mint*:

Papaya has been used for bad infections. Externally, the fruit, pressed against the problem eats and digests the infection. Used internally it digests things too. The taste of *Papaya* and *Mint* is good. Kids like to open the capsules and eat two or three with their meals.

Betain and *Pepsin*:

This is *Hydrochloric Acid* found naturally in a healthy stomach to digest proteins. When I eat a meat meal I take one or two. Some people take them with every meal.

Food Enzymes:

Obtainable at any good health food store.

Enzymes cover it all. Everything is here to digest whatever is eaten.

I've had people tell me they felt physically healthy in all ways after the first day of taking one to three tablets with each meal.

Continued...

Stomach Upheavals

The Flatulent Flatterer

"Come on," Elaine said to me, "I know this very exclusive, rich place where all the beautiful people go. Let's go check it out and see how 'Single Land' lives."

"OK," I agreed. "I want to meet some of these gorgeous guys with gold-plated lives."

We went. You know what happened? This perfectly proper, nice-looking man spent several hours charming me. He described his stomach in detail. He complained bitterly about the gas and wind he was experiencing and took me on a turn around the dance floor. His wind blew several lady's skirts up. He finally excused himself and went home. Big evening! He should have taken a remedy that historically helps food digest and prevents heartburn.

Combination B-24
Papaya Fruit
Ginger Root
Peppermint Leaves   Useful with gas, heartburn and indiges-
Wild Yam Root
Fennel Seeds   tion.
Lobelia Herb
Spearmint Leaves
Catnip Herb

A little *Ginger* in his pocket would have come in handy too.

Building and Cleansing

You're all excited about herbs. Now that you know, or suspect that you're full of worms and poisons, you want to jump right in and clean out the mess. You want to ream out your bowel, strip your blood, flush those kidneys, shovel out the bladder, dump those lungs, dig out those ears, rinse the sinus, unclog the prostate and just generally get things moving.

Don't. I can almost guarantee that every hole in your body will open up and pour forth. Within two days, two weeks or two months, you will say, "This is a bad deal. I hate my herbalist. I'm going to give up this messy hobby and find another." I know. I did it to myself when I didn't know what I was doing. (Read my book, *The Outrageous Herb Lady*).

From my **exciting experience** I worked out a plan that you may wish to follow. It looks like this:

Half Build—Half Cleanse

A *Cleansing* herb, or combination, is one that cleanses the body.

A *Building* herb, or combination, is one that repairs and strengthens the body.

See the Appendix at the back of the book for my list of *Cleansers* and *Builders*. You may disagree with some of them, but I'm writing this book so what I say goes.

B stands for *Builder*.

C stands for *Cleanser*.

BC stands for *Builder* and *Cleanser*.

All of the combinations I mention can be bought already mixed in capsules, or you can put them together yourself. All the suggested uses are historical or traditional, of course.

For comfort **half cleanse** and **half build** (or build more than you cleanse.)

PLUS

Work on one major problem.

A basic starter program might be:

One *Cleanser* (perhaps a bowel cleanser like **Combination C-6**)[6]

6. See Appendix I

AND

One *Builder* (maybe one to build and repair tissues like ***Combination B-1***)[7]

OR

A single *Builder* like *Bee Pollen*

Then sit down and think, "What can I fix before it kills me? What's my most pressing problem?" Maybe it's your heart. You would choose several herbs or combinations traditionally used to repair that organ, like *Hawthorn,* a good *mineral combination* and *Chlorophyll.*

This would give you a starter program like this:

Starter Program

One cleanser like ***Combination C-6***:

> *Combination C-6*
> *Cascara Sagrada Bark*
> *Buckthorn Bark*
> *Licorice Root*
> *Capsicum Fruit*   Bowel Cleanser
> *Ginger Root*
> *Barberry Rootbark*
> *Couch-grass Herb*
> *Red Clover Tops*
> *Lobelia Herb*

One builder like *Bee Pollen* or ***Combination B-1***:

> *Combination B-1*
> *Comfrey Root*
> *Alfalfa Herb*
> *Oat Straw*   Tissue and nerve repair
> *Irish Moss Plant*
> *Horsetail Herb*
> *Lobelia Herb*

Plus herbs for one major problem. For example, heart:
   Hawthorn
   Mineral Combination
   Chlorophyll

Maybe you'd like to add another cleanser? Fine. But be sure you add another *Builder*[8] to balance. If you don't you may feel extra rotten and weak from all the cleansing. You can build an elaborate structure into this program by adding *Cleansers* for any organ, plus *Builders,* plus work on different ailments.

---

7. See Appendix I
8. See Appendix I

PART II

How I Take Herbs

A man too busy to take care of his health is like a mechanic too busy to take care of his tools

Spanish Proverb

How I Take Herbs

So herbs sound good to you. But where do you start? First decide **what** you want to do for yourself. (If it's a friend or a relative you are worried about, try to get their full cooperation.) Then decide how you're going to do it.

The Simple Sissies Program

After some of you finish this section on how I take herbs you may say, "Wowee! I could never take herbs like that! I'd never get 'em all down and it must cost a fortune, anyway." First off, herbs don't cost a fortune. They average about six or seven dollars a bottle. Some less, some more. If you get 100 capsules to the bottle they can last you from one month to three, depending on your personal needs.

Add up the cost of a regular size herbal regime. You'll find it costs much less than a visit to a doctor with prescriptions included. Not only that, those of us who are faithful herb users almost never see doctors or hospitals. You can't beat the cost in peace of mind.

If some of you are intrigued by herbs but want to start with just a big toe's worth, here's a simple program:

The Simple Sissies Sample Program

1. Choose any *Bowel Cleansing Combination.*[9] A simple bowel cleanser can often bring about dramatic changes.
   Approximate cost: $9 per bottle
2. Choose any *Builder* or *Combination of same.*[10]
   Approximate cost: $6.50 per bottle.
   Total cost: $15.50

If the capsules last only one month that's about 51 cents a day. What does your health insurance cost you per day? For herbal health insurance 51 cents per day is **much** less expensive than paper coverage and feels better.

If I were basically healthy I'd slowly work through a cleansing and building program. As I mentioned earlier, I'd probably start with a bowel cleanser along with a *Builder* and maybe work on a weak area. With me ... female problems.

9. See Appendix I
10. See Appendix I

My Beginning Sample Herb Program

	Cleansers	**Builders**	
Bowel Cleanser	**Combination C-6** Cascara Sagrada Bark Buckthorn Bark Licorice Root Capsicum Fruit Ginger Fruit Ginger Root Barberry Rootbark Couch-grass Herb Red Clover Tops Lobelia Herb	**Combination B-17** Black Cohosh Root Capsicum Fruit Valerian Root Mistletoe Herb Lady's Slipper Root Lobelia Herb Skullcap Herb Hops Flowers Wood Betony Herb	Nerve Repair
Bowel Cleanser	**Combination C-9** Psyllium Hulls Hibiscus Flower Licorice Root	Alfalfa Concentrate	Builder— Supplies Nutrients

Combination C-6 is my **Cleanser** of choice. I've chosen one of the bowel cleansers.

Combination B-17 is a **Builder**. It's a good one for me because I tend to be nervous and need some work on nerve repair.

Combination C-9 is another good *Cleanser, Psyllium Hulls*. I want this because I tend to have pockets in my bowel and want to clean them out.

Alfalfa Concentrate is another *Builder*. It has lots of vitamins, minerals and trace elements. I could have chosen any other *Builder*. I just didn't.

Now, I've got two *Builders* to balance two *Cleansers*. I think I'll add something for one of my **major** health problems which happens to be a hormone imbalance.

Combination B-5 Golden Seal Root Red Rasberry Leaves Black Cohosh Root Queen of the Meadow Herb Marshmellow Root Blessed Thistle Herb Lobelia Herb Capsicum Fruit Ginger Root	Hormone Balance

Combination B-5 is a *Builder* and balances female hormones.

Remember...I can have more *Builders* than *Cleansers*, but not the other way around.

After I've gotten going real good, I'll keep working on some basic problems and switch around on others.

If I were basically dying, I'd hit things harder.

I'm still taking all the herbs from my *"Beginning Sample Herb Program."* It's a month later and I add to, and work on, a few other areas.

I add a *Blood Cleanser,* **Combination C-1.**

I've felt a little tired so I'm adding a *Builder* that provides instant energy and also builds my body, **Combination B-10.**

If I haven't already done so, I add **Combination B-19.** This is a *Builder* for my thyroid. It's also a combination that helps regulate the glandular system.

Blood Cleanser	**Combination C-1** Yellow Dock Root Dandelion Root Burdock Root Licorice Root Chaparral Herb Red Clover Tops Barberry Rootbark Cascara Sagrada Bark Yarrow Herb Sarsaparilla Root	**Combination B-10** Capsicum Fruit Siberian Ginseng Root Gotu Kola Herb **Combination B-19** Kelp Plant Irish Moss Plant Parsley Herb Capsicum Fruit	Energy Thyroid

At this point I'm taking eight different kinds of capsules. You may think that's a lot when you see them in front of you, but it isn't. I know people who take more herbs than that.

I have purposely omitted the number of capsules of each combination, or single herb, that I take. The reason I did that is because amounts are an individual matter. We will cover how to determine amounts later.

Two or three weeks later I might add a combination to **clean** and **build** my liver. Plus a *Building Combination* for thick hair, pretty skin and strong nails:

To Build and Cleanse the Liver	**Combination BC-3** Red Beet Root Dandelion Root Parsley Herb Horsetail (Shavegrass) Herb Liverwort Herb Birch Leaves	Lobelia Herb Blessed Thistle Herb Angelica Root Chamomile Flowers Gentian Root Golden Rod Herb
For pretty hair, skin and nails	**Combination B-33** Dulse Horsetail Sage Rosemary	

One month or two after starting my herb program, my *Sample Herb Program* will look like this:

My Sample Herb Program #1

Bowel
Cleanser

Combination C-6
Cascara Sagrada Bark
Buckthorn Bark
Licorice Root
Capsicum Fruit
Ginger Root
Barberry Rootbark
Couch-grass Herb
Red Clover Tops
Lobelia Herb

Combination C-9
Psyllium Hulls
Hibiscus Flower
Licorice Root

Bowel
Cleanser

Blood
Cleanser

Combination C-1
Yellow Dock Root
Dandelion Root
Burdock Root
Licorice Root
Chaparral Herb
Red Clover Tops
Barberry Rootbark
Cascara Sagrada Bark
Yarrow Herb
Sarsaparilla Root

Combination BC-3
Red Beet Root
Dandelion Root
Parsley Herb
Horsetail (Shavegrass) Herb
Liverwort Herb
Birch Leaves
Lobelia Herb
Blessed Thistle Herb
Angelica Root
Chamomile Flowers
Gentian Root
Golden Rod Herb

Liver Cleanser
and Builder

Nerve Builder

Combination B-17
Black Cohosh Root
Capsicum Fruit
Valerian Root
Mistletoe Herb
Lady's Slipper Root
Lobelia Herb
Skullcap Herb
Hops Flowers
Wood Betony Herb

Continued...

Builder	*Alfalfa Concentrate*	
	Combination B-10 *Capsicum Fruit* *Siberian Ginseng Root* *Gotu Kola Herb*	Energy Builder
Thyroid Builder	**Combination B-19** *Kelp Plant* *Irish Moss Plant* *Parsley Herb* *Capsicum Fruit*	
	Combination B-5 *Golden Seal Root* *Red Raspberry Leaves* *Black Cohosh Root* *Queen of the Meadow Herb* *Marshmallow Root* *Blessed Thistle Herb* *Lobelia Herb* *Capsicum Fruit* *Ginger Root*	Hormone Balancer
For the Hair Skin and Nails	**Combination B-33** *Dulse* *Horsetail* *Sage* *Rosemary*	

I'll stay on this program for maybe four to six months. Then I'll take a look at it and say, "OK is there anything I can **stop** taking? Anything I should add?

First of all I started with cleaning my bowel. That takes at least a year for the average person, so I can't cut that out. I can change the herbs, however. Maybe I'll stop taking the one I'm taking for the bowel and take another bowel cleanser like, **Combination C-5.** This one has a good reputation for killing parasites, too. I'd leave in **Combination C-9,** the *Psyllium Hulls.*

I've been taking the herbal nerve **Combination B-17.** I think I'll switch it for another herbal combination like **Combination B-16.** This is a *Builder.*

Please Note: It's a good idea to trade back and forth on many of the herbs and combinations. If you don't they may not keep working for you. The body gets used to the same old thing and doesn't do as well with it.

Now I look at the *Builders* I've been taking. I think I'll stop the *Alfalfa Concentrate* and begin taking *Bee Pollen.*

I've been taking the herbal nerve **Combination B-17.** I think I'll switch it for another herbal nerve combination like **Combination B-16.** This is a *Builder.*

26

Might as well change *Blood Cleansers* too. I'll stop the one I'm taking, **Combination C-1,** and try **Combination C-2.**

I'll stop taking **Combination B-10** and exchange it for another energy builder, **Combination B-9.**

Instead of using **Combination B-19** to build my thyroid I'll exchange it for **Combination B-20,** which does the same thing.

I might as well exchange my liver *Cleanser* and *Builder* too. I'll stop taking **Combination BC-3** and start taking **Combination BC-4.**

(When you're doing this you might want to write out your herbal program on a long piece of paper so you can keep track of what the hector you're doing.)

Gradually, I will be able to stop taking many of these and work on other parts of my body. Or, if I can handle it, I'll just add in more capsules of other herbs.[11]

Four to **six** months later my *Sample Herb Program* will look like this:

My Sample Herb Program #2

Bowel Cleanser	**Combination C-5** Pumpkin Seeds Culver's Root Mandrake Root Violet Leaves Comfrey Root Cascara Sagrada Bark Witch Hazel Bark Mullein Leaves Slippery Elm Bark	**Combination BC-4** Barberry Root Bark Ginger Root Cramp Bark Fennel Seeds Peppermint Leaves Wild Yam Root Catnip Herb	Liver Cleanser and Builder
Bowel Cleanser	**Combination C9** Psyllium Hulls Hibiscus Flower Licorice Root	**Combination B-16** Black Cohosh Root Capsicum Fruit Valerian Root Mistletoe Herb Ginger Root	Nerve Builder
Blood Cleanser	**Combination C-3** Licorice Root Red Clover Tops Sarsaparilla Root Cascara Sagrada Bark Oregon Grape Root Chaparral Herb Burdock Root Buckthorn Bark Prickly Ash Bark Peach Bark Stillingia Root	St. Johnswort Herb Hops Flowers Wood Betony Herb Bee Pollen	Builder Continued...

---

11. For more guidance on how to use these herbs and combinations, refer to:
    a. *Little Herb Encyclopedia,* Dr. Jack Ritchason
    b. *Today's Herbal Health,* Louise Tenney
    c. *Herbally Yours,* Penny C. Royal

Builder	**Combination B-9** *Siberian Ginseng Rootbark* *Ho Shou-Wu Root* *Black Walnut Hulls* *Licorice Root* *Gentain Root* *Comfrey Root* *Fennel Seeds* *Bee Pollen* *Bayberry Rootbark* *Myrrh Gum* *Peppermint Leaves* *Safflower Flowers* *Eucalyptus Leaves* *Lemongrass Herb* *Capsicum Fruit*	
	Combination B-20 *Irish Moss Plant* *Kelp Plant* *Black Walnut Hulls* *Parsley Herb* *Watercress Herb* *Sarsaparilla Root* *Iceland Moss Plant*	Thyroid Builder
Hormone Balancer	**Combination B-6** *Golden Seal Root* *Capsicum Fruit* *False Unicorn Root* *Ginger Root* *Uva Ursi Leaves* *Cramp Bark* *Squaw Vine Herb* *Blessed Thistle Herb* *Red Raspberry Leaves*	
	Combination B-33 *Dulse* *Horsetail* *Sage* *Rosemary*	For the Hair, Skin and Nails Continue taking this one.
Energy Builder	**Combination B-10** *Capsicum Fruit* *Siberian Ginseng Root* *Gotu Kola Herb*	

Amounts to Take

Taking seven to eight different herbs per day plus vitamins and minerals is an easy program for me. More often I read about a terrific new herb and **have** to try it. The next day I may read about another one I have to try and so on until I'm taking a cereal bowl full.

Concentrated Herbs

Some herb companies have herbs that have bulk and moisture removed. The essence of the herb is left, four to six times more potent than the unconcentrated herbs. I take these whenever possible.

Starting Out

When starting an herbal program, I begin slowly. I don't take the recommended amount the first day. If you get good quality herbs you may get gas, cramping, stomach upsets, diarrhea, headaches, etc. Daily, I increase the number of herbs until I'm taking the recommended amount. If at some point I'm feeling too obnoxious and ill from toxic stir-up I cut back on the herbs to where my symptoms are tolerable. You can control your symptoms.

Just **remember**! Herbs do not cover symptoms! They bring the problem **out** of the body.

A while back, a lady with a dreadful sinus infection came to see me. She said her sinuses would let loose in the night and she felt she was drowning in sea water. As long as she used a nosesquirt she didn't drain but she felt like a rotten pumpkin. She collected a few herbs and went home.

Several nights later this lady called, frantic. My 12-year-old daughter, Summer, answered the phone as I wasn't home.

"Help!" the woman pleaded. "I took those herbs and I'm worse than ever. I'm pouring mucus from my eyes and nose and I have a terrible cold. I'm sick!"

Calmly, Summer assured her that was wonderful.

"It is?" the lady asked.

"Of course," Summer went on. "You've got to expect this. It's a wonderful sign. If **I** felt too bad, **I** would just cut back on the herb amounts."

"Oh, really?" the lady asked meekly. "Isn't that nice, then? I'll call you back in a few days if I don't get well." She never called back.

Don't be afraid of symptoms while on herbs, no matter how bizarre.

Often when you first start you will spend a lot of time sweating and smelling foul. But remember my axiom, "better **out** than **in**," right?

And don't feel disappointed if you don't feel bad or run rivers of toxins. A lot of people feel better than they ever have in their lives. Others feel tremendous until they have a healing crisis when they're sure they're dying, or at least getting no better. Then they have an upswing and realize they feel better than good.

With herbs it seems to be three steps forward, one back. Three steps up, one back. Be patient. Any good herbalist will tell you to stay with an herbal program for at least six months before you decide if you're better or worse.

"Oh, but..." you may say, "It's so hard to keep taking all those herbs and vitamins. I forget."

Try this: It takes 21 days to form a new habit. Promise yourself that for 21 days, **solid**, you will take those herbs at specified times. After 21 days I think you will find yourself taking those herbs without giving it a second thought. After that, try taking your supplements only six days a week. This gives you one certain day (Sunday is nice) to let you and your body rest. The herbs and vitamins will work better too. Everybody and everything needs a day off once a week.

"Those Herbs are Stuck!"

Have you noticed how sometimes all those herbs seem to get stuck in your throat and hold a convention? Or it feels like they're grouped in your ribs, stomach, even your back? You feel a burning sensation, a coldness or a lump? You grab your throat and your eyes bulge? You're sure you're going to be the first person to die from swallowing capsules, right? The first time it happened to me, I'd casually swallowed about 10, or so, one right after the other, and gone on fixing dinner. Suddenly, I stiffened and grabbed the left side of my lower back. In some incredible fashion all the herbs seemed to have taken a bus tour to watch my kidneys flush. Waves of alarming sensations washed from my back to my throat. Those herbs were all taking an elevator ride to watch my tonsils hang. I threw down the spatula and raced onto the back patio. It was dark and it was cold, but I was dying so what did it matter? I paced back and forth the length of the patio. The unique, undulating sensations continued as I alternately grabbed my back and throat. My eyes pressed out of my head, my tongue hung. I suffered and sweated. My family was right inside, but I never like to bother them when I'm dying. Gradually my symptoms subsided and I returned to finish dinner. The family never knew they almost lost me.

If this ever happens to you, first of all you'll live. Second, here's how to prevent or stop the feeling. Take fewer capsules at a time and space them out a bit. Take them with food in your stomach. If you get to feeling weird anyway, take a teaspoon of *salad oil* or some *raw parsley* or *tomato juice.* An instant miracle happens. No more sensations.

Determining Dosages

When it comes to how many capsules or amounts of herbs you should take, everyone is different. I always start slowly and watch, to see what happens. Some people are like delicate little flowers. They need very small amounts to get results. One lady took one capsule of a bowel cleanser and had diarrhea for four days. She couldn 't even go to work. Others I've known have had to take thirty to forty capsules and even then needed an earthquake to jar them loose. If you're taking bottled herbs in capsules the manufacturer usually has the suggested amount to take on the back. That gives you a general idea. Maybe we can liken it to going to a buffet. You can put a dab of this and a little dollop of that on your plate; go moderate or pile the plate straight up. Whatever you need.

Read the following story and remember it whenever you're tempted to be too enthusiastic in your herb program:

Cross Country Runs

Dan the Trucker told me this one:

"I had a three day run to make from San Diego to Texas. My chiropractor had given me some of your herbs. The ones to get rid of worms. You know. *Black Walnut.* Well, he said, 'take six capsules a day, Dan.' But I was goin' on this here run, see, and I knew I wouldn't take 'em on the road. So, I says to myself, 'Make it easy guy. Take 'em **all** before you leave.' So I did. The day I left, I took 18 of those babies all at once.

"The second day of the drive I noticed I was feelin' a little uncomfortable. A little gas, you know. Pretty soon my guts started roiling mighty bad. Well, heck, I was steaming down the road here and no time to stop. I just lifted my rear a little to relieve the pressure. Pass some gas, right? Holy moly! I lifted my rear and Woosh! Splat! I passed more than air! It splattered all over the inside of my jeans and down my legs. I was horrified. Only it didn't stop there. Everytime I let gas it happened. By the time I saw a rest area I was soaked and mad as hell!

"I screeched my truck into that rest stop and was out the door and running.

"I shot into the bathroom. I musta' spent two hours there and another fifteen minutes dunking my jeans and shorts in the toilet. Then, there I stood stark naked except for my shirt, shoes and socks. I darted out the door with those damn jeans against my privates and scurried to my truck. Back on the road, I came to a weigh station. I told the guy in charge, 'Weigh the truck. I'm not getting out. Don't you dare ask why.'

"I had to drive 300 miles like that. Bare-assed."

Muscle Testing

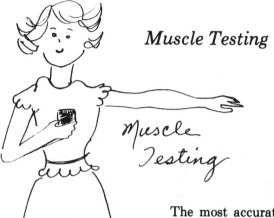

The most accurate and fun way to find exact amounts is to use muscle testing.

When I'm feeling off, a little scratchy around the edges, or have burrs in my aura, I call in my daughter and ask her to muscle test me.

I begin by placing one fist on my chest, the other arm held out to my side. Summer then presses on my outstretched wrist (not too hard) and says, "Resist me, Mom." We get a feel for my strength. Then with my right hand I hold a bottle of herbs or vitamins against my chest. She presses my wrist again. If I weaken, even slightly, that's not the herb for me (at least not at this time). If I stay the same, it's OK. If I feel stronger, my body is crying for that one. To prove the validity of this, hold a box of sugar against your chest. Most people will weaken automatically. If by some chance you find someone who strengthens on sugar, ask if they are under great stress. If they are under tremendous stress the adrenals will be grateful for anything.

The test I just described is fine, but I like this one better. It's easier and more fun. Make a circle with your thumb and forefinger. Have someone take their two forefingers, tell you to resist and attempt to pull your thumb and finger apart. This tests your strength. If the person being tested is too strong, use one of their weaker fingers to oppose the thumb. Purists will probably scream at this, but it works just as well for me. Now take your right hand and place in it whatever you're testing. A plastic bottle of herbs or vitamins works fine for me. Things in metal containers may not work. Now, have your friend try to pull your finger and thumb apart once more, using medium pressure. If you weaken it's **not** for you. Some products will make you stronger. You can even use this method to test **amounts** of herbs and vitamins the body can use. I have someone pour 20 capsules, or so, in my right hand.

Generally I test weak on that many (but not always). The other person keeps removing capsules one at a time, until I test strong again.

Each time they test, they say, "Testing to see how many of this Venus needs today." It's amazing. Just remember it's not a contest of who's stronger. You don't have to use all 100 pounds of muscle when you test someone.

If you want to explore this fascinating subject for yourself there are several excellent books on the subject. These are some I've read:

Healing Energies, Dr. Stephen P. Shepard
Your Body Doesn't Lie, Dr. John Diamond
Touch For Health, John Thie, D.C. and Mary Marks, D.C.
Muscle Response Test, Dr. Walter Fischman and Dr. Mark Grinims
The Body Says Yes, Pricilla Kapell

Babies and Children

Little kids generally need less than an adult because they're smaller. If I were taking six capsules of *Catnip,* for example, I might give my baby one or two. Again, you can use muscle testing on children, even if they're too young to cooperate. There's a method called *"surrogate testing*[12].*"* This will astound you, but when two people touch they exchange energies. (This should give you something to think about.) To test a baby, test his mother first, or someone close to the child. She should test strong. Then have her touch the baby and you can test the baby by testing her. It's amazing to see how this works. You can even test animals this way or people who are bed-ridden.

12. *Touch For Health,* John Thie D.C. and Mary Marks D.C.
   The Body Says Yes, Pricilla Kapell

"When Do I Take Herbs?"

To obtain maximum benefits from herbs and vitamins, I take one third with breakfast, one third with lunch and one third with dinner. I take them just before or after a meal.

You only eat once a day? Well, just take them whenever then. How about with a glass of tomato juice? They can't help you if they stay in the bottle. I like to take mine in liquid *Chlorophyll* mixed with water. *Chlorophyll* seems to help pull the nutrients into the cells.

"How Do I Get Herbs Down Babies, Kids, My Husband?"

With babies and kids you can mix the powdered herbs in apple sauce, jam, honey, molasses or their food. You can put garlic powder on buttered toast. You can pay them a dollar a pill to learn to swallow capsules. Or you can get really callous and grease and insert them up their bottoms. The herbs work just as well that way.

With husbands it's a bit harder. You might invest in plastic vitamin packets (found in some health food stores) or tiny Tupperware holders. Put each day's herbs in them so they're easy to take. Or you can be sneaky and hide herbs in their food or drink. *Aloe Vera Juice* hides nicely in apple or other fruit juices.

One day my brother, Jim, told me quite emphatically that he, no way, would **ever**, under any circumstances, take *Aloe Vera Juice*! His wife spoke up, "That's real interesting, Jim. You've been taking it for two months in your apple juice."

"How Can I Help Others With Herbs?"

You've taken herbs and gotten good results. You're enthusiastic. You want to tell everyone who will listen and even those who won't. First of all remember your family is not the place to start. They've known you all your life and know you don't know anything. Strangers are ideal. They don't know you and believe you know what you're talking about.

If you want to help people get healthy naturally I think you should keep your major vices hidden. Don't be a saint, but you don't need to be excessively human either. For example, I trained one lady in the herbs but she wasn't making much impression on her friends. I suggested, "Sally, get a group together at your house and I'll come over and give a lecture. That way I'll see why your friends aren't responding."

The evening of the class came. I walked in Sally's front door. Her entire living room was decorated with empty whiskey bottles! Sally chain-smoked through the class and served robust rounds of coffee, doughnuts and sugar cookies.

Later I tactfully suggested, in so many words, "Don't be a hypocrite, but it's a good idea to practice what you preach."

When taking herbs you may be so pleased about the results you'll feel like Marion, who told me, "I've got my ex-husband on all the herbs, and we're not even friends."

"How Can I Find Good Quality Herbs?"

I used to be quite sick.[13] After thirty years of it, I sat down and started diagnosing and treating myself. From all the books I'd read, I was convinced that **herbs** were **the** answer. I trotted excitedly to the health food store and stocked up. After a month of taking those herbs nothing had happened. Nothing. Fortunately, while in the depths of depression from this latest failure, I was introduced to a powerful, top quality line of herbs.[14] They worked. I could tell the difference between herb brands within days. Now, they are the only ones I use and carry in my herb shop.

Remembering that you may be an unknowing bimbo off the street like I was, let me give you some guidelines. First, you might buy several or more brands of the **same** herb. Take one brand for four or five days. Wait a few days, then try another brand. Notice how or what you feel. Most people who get herbs from me call and say, "Wow! I've taken herbs for a long time, but I really feel the difference with the ones you gave me."

Be aware that there are hustlers and low guys even in the health food field. The *Aloe Vera Juice* you're buying is low cost, tastes good and says it's 100 percent pure *Aloe Vera*. Well, sure, the amount that's in there may be pure *Aloe Vera*, but how about all the water? And the additives? And is the plant at least four years old?

Does your brand of herbs use cold processing so the herb is still alive and kicking? Or do they use heat? Is the most medicinal part of the herb used or the cheaper part? It goes on and on.

You might try muscle testing different brands. In my shop, people like to bring in various brands of herbs, vitamins, foods, drugs, whatever. We have fun testing them. Almost invariably the brand that cured me tests well for them. Consequently, I've ended up with a heavy mail-order business sending herbs and vitamins all over the United States.

13. *The Outrageous Herb Lady,* Venus Catherine Andrecht
14. *The Outrageous Herb Lady,* Venus Catherine Andrecht

Capsules, Teas or Roll Your Own

When I first started herbs I did it the cheap way. I thought. I stood in my kitchen for hours with a bowl of empty capsules and a bag of powdered *Black Cohosh*. I ended up covered with flying herb powder and gummy messes all over my sink counter. The capsules got moist from my feverish attention, stuck together and infuriated me. I figured up the expense and realized I'd spent more than the bottled, encapsulated herbs would have cost.

If you like *Capsicum* powder on your chin and under your armpits, I recommend encapsulating your own. Otherwise, I'd stick to ready-made. For another thing, the herb isn't sitting loose in a jar losing its potency.

As for teas, they're quite nice and comforting. Babies like them. But again, teas tend to lose their strength rather quickly. I'd stick to capsules.

"How Long Will My Herbs Stay Potent?"

Keep your herbs tightly capped, out of direct sunlight and in cool places. If you treat them well herbs should last two to three years, at least. Extracts and tinctures remain potent much longer.

"What Can I Expect From Taking Herbs And How Soon?"

Everyone wants me to look them in the eye and say, "In two days you will be well. In three days you will have the strength, body and lusty nature of Tarzan. In four days you will be bone-chillingly beautiful. Guaranteed!"

Can't say it...Can't do it.

Here's what I've seen happen:

Most people feel something within the first week or two. Some feel so much better they're clapping and kissing me. Some feel cruddy. Some think they don't feel enough. A few feel nothing.

After one and a half months changes may be more noticeable. Often by six months they will stand and tell me, bald-faced, that they never were sick in the first place. Or, never were flat chested, or their nails never broke and they always had sweet dispositions.

"How Long Do I Have To Take These Things?"

When a person feels better they're often tempted to quit their herbs and vitamins. Don't! Your body is like a bank account. Many of us have withdrawn all our money. We're bouncing checks. With herbs you put money back into the account and bring it to a healthy balance. Then you've got to keep putting some money in as you pay your daily bills.

"Can I Keep Eating All My Junk?"

Some people sit across from me at my desk. They clutch their bags of herbs and their lips droop and tremble a bit. "Do I hafta..." they whine. "Change my diet to make these work?" They give me a plaintive look. "I don't want to stop my coffee and cigarettes. I guess I should, huh? What do you think, huh? There's nothing else I need to cut out, right?"

Here's the straight story friends. I have seen coffee-drinking, tobacco-smoking, junk-eating, perverted sugar-holics get well while taking herbs. I'm always dumbfounded. I turn to my herbs and shake my head. "Well, you little guys...you really are a marvel!"

However, this does not mean it will work for **you**. If you help the herbs they will help you even more. Here are the same old boring guidelines. They never change: A box of chocolate cookies with banana frosting and sugar sprinkles never sneaks in as OK.

No: White flour products. White sugar. Canned goods. Packaged goods. Additives. Coffee. Tea. Alcohol. Sodas or Processed foods.

But listen, I'm not mean. Ease into this. Do everything in moderation. Start by cutting back on some things. Be good to yourself. Have a little wine before dinner, if you must. If you slobber everytime you see an ice cream bar, don't suffer, eat one. When people jump into a new way of life, such as a strict-strict diet, after a while they totally fall apart and quit all their good intentions, or they continue with it and become absolutely insufferable. So bend a little.

37

Herbs Versus Drugs

Mrs. "D." had a nameless illness. Her family spent $6000 for tests and more tests and still she couldn't hold anything in her stomach. She'd been in the hospital for weeks. Finally a friend took her a bottle of an herbal coffee. The sick woman took the whole bottle the first night and held it down. The next day she took another. Mrs. "D." felt the herbs did more for her at $4 than $6000 worth of testing.

We've been brought up to believe that chemicals (drugs) will cure us, or if not, make us more comfortable to the end (or more miserable to the end). That's where herbs differ from drugs. Drugs, generally, just cover up **symptoms** while you're riding merrily on the road to your demise. Herbs do **not** cover up **symptoms**. Herbs attempt to **reverse** the process of bodily disintegration. Herbs are specific foods which contain elements the sick body may be lacking. The body takes what it needs and uses it to repair itself.

The idea of drugs being mainly dangerous or useless, or merely palliative may sound heretical to you. But that's because you're too young to remember. For most of recorded history herbs have been the only, or a major method, of healing. Don't let people or articles tell you that because of modern medicine we're the healthiest people in the world. That's propaganda.

At this writing, some people feel the United States should be rated about 95 in world health. Civilization may have advanced in trauma care and surgical procedures, but when it comes to the **quality** of our lives there's no reason to wave celebration flags.

Up until about 100 years ago, and even less, herbs were used regularly in this country.

Herbs have many advantages:
1. They're all natural
2. They're inexpensive
3. They have few, if any harmful side-effects
4. There's little danger of an overdose
5. You don't need a prescription for them

With Medical Drugs you get:
1. High cost
2. Side-effects
3. High possibility of overdoses and misuse
4. Need for prescriptions

What disturbs me most are the devasting side-effects from drugs. A great many people in hospitals are there because of drug induced ailments. I've seen many people whose bodies have been damaged by medical drugs. You can call the destruction by any disease name you wish. These disruptions range all the way from the most minor, such as violent rear end itch from too much coffee drinking (caffeine is a drug) to destroyed body organs.

Can I Mix Herbs With Drugs?

Almost everyone I know who goes to an herbalist is taking medications. They're on thyroid pills, heart pills, high blood pressure pills, water pills and "I don't know what it's for" pills. Their first question is:

"Can I take these herbs with my drugs?"

My answer is, "Herbs are plants. Foods. Some drugs don't mix well with foods. For example, your doctor may tell you not to drink milk with your antibiotic because the antibiotic is neutrilized. I use the same logic. I'd take my herbs and drugs at different times. Maybe an hour apart. I've known thousands of people who've taken both and never had any problems.

Should I Stop Taking My Drugs?

Holy George, **NO**. Your body may have become dependent on them. One lady decided, on her own, to stop taking her thyroid pills once she started the thyroid building herbs. The sudden loss of the chemical her body had come to rely on made her feel crazy.

Also, those drugs just might be keeping you alive. You don't want to drop dead do you? You'd make herbal healing look real bad and we'd all be pretty upset with you. Many people just start taking their herbs and sit tight. Then, after a few weeks they **gradually** start cutting back on their drugs a bit and see how they feel. Eventually, many people find they're able to chuck their drugs altogether.

PART III

Herbs Historically Used For Those Common Everyday Problems

"The first wealth is health. Sickness is poor-spirited and cannot serve anyone; it must husband its resources to live. But health answers its own ends and has to spare; runs over and inundates the neighborhoods and creeks of other men's necessities."

Emerson

Colds, Flus, Sore Throats And Infections

Good Try

Ludmilla, an herbalist from Montana, told me this one.

It was about midnight when I felt someone shaking my shoulder. I drifted up from sleep and came eye to eye with my husband, Isaac. The light was on and he was clutching his throat. His eyebrows were moving frantically up and down.

"What's the matter with you?" I asked. His mouth opened wide. He loosened his hold from my arm and pointed his finger into his mouth.

"Are you choking?" I asked. He shook his head no and jabbed his finger at his neck.

"Does it start with a C?" I queried. He shook his head. "M?" I asked.

He made a mad face and rasped, "I have a sore throat! I want to go to the hospital!"

I cocked my head. "For a sore throat? At midnight? No way!" I gave him a disapproving scowl. "Haven't you ever had a sore throat before, Isaac?"

He lay back on the bed with a moan. "I've never had one like this. I'm dying!"

"Open your mouth," I said. He did and I peered in. "Your tongue is in the way." I reached in a drawer for the flashlight, turned and pried open his mouth. Everything looked the same to me. No swelling, no redness. I sat back and looked at him.

He moaned and repeated, "I want to go to the hospital."

"Are you kidding?" I asked. "I'm an herb lady. I'll fix you up." (This was a number of years ago when I first started studying herbs and fancied I knew a few things.)

"What you need," I said with authority, "Is a gargle." I ran downstairs, drew some warm water and collected various herbs. Then I carefully mixed a concoction. Upstairs again I led Isaac, protesting all the way, to the bathroom. He gargled. No change. Well, then, he could just swallow a handful of herbs! He did. No change. I was expecting an instant miracle. Isaac limped back to bed, complaining all the way.

He'd "never had a sore throat like this!" I was "cruel!" "Some wife" I was. I "wouldn't even take him to the hospital."

"Lie down," I said. "I'm not through yet." I whipped out an herb book, flipped a few pages. Ah, here it was. I'd been wanting to try this one, but hadn't had the opportunity. I eyed Isaac. Now I did. "It says here," I began, "to take a hot, wet, salted towel and wrap it around the neck of a sore throat sufferer. Are you up for that?"

"Anything," he mumbled.

"Oh boy!" I dashed into the bathroom for a towel. All I could find were big bath towels. One would have to do. I ran a sink full of hot water and dropped in the towel. Then squished it around. Pulled it out. Boy, was that a lot of wet towel!

"I can't let it cool off," I whispered. I gave a hasty squeeze. I raced to the bed, grabbed Isaac's head from the pillow and slung the slopping wet towel around his neck. He looked startled, but trusting. I gave it several wrap arounds, the darn towel was that long. The bed was sopping wet. Isaac was sopping wet. Too late now. I stood back to look. Oh my gosh! I'd forgotten to salt the towel. I ran and got a big salt shaker and thundered back upstairs. Isaac lay quietly as I salted him. And salted some more. I stood back to assess the situation. Salting someone seemed like a crazy idea to me.

"Feel better?" I asked, hopefully.

"No," Isaac said.

I crossed my arms and breathed a while. I looked at the clock, then back at Isaac. "I've been at this two hours," I said. "I tell you what," I climbed back into bed and pulled the covers up. "You're either going to live or you're going to die. I'm going to sleep."

He lived.

Ludmilla added, "We realized later the sore throat had come from some herbs that traditionally clear the sinuses. They were working and he was draining an acrid discharge."

I've found that gargling *Apple Cider Vinegar* works well for sore throats. So does a *Garlic* clove cut in half and held in the mouth. Of course it keeps people away, but you don't want to infect your friends, anyway. Straight *Lemon Juice* gargled is helpful. Of course *Lemon Juice* has *Vitamin A* and *Vitamin C*. (Some viruses respond to *Vitamin C* but not to *Vitamin A* and vice versa.)

Herbal Helpers

Combination C-10
Echinacea Root
Golden Seal Root
Yarrow Flowers
Capsicum Fruit

This historically fights infection.

Combination C-16
Comfrey Root
Marshmallow Root
Mullein Leaves
Slippery Elm Bark
Lobelia Herb

Deep cleans the lungs and sinuses.

Continued...

Combination C-18
Comfrey Root
Fenugreek Seeds

Whenever I take this I bring up a lot of mucus.

Combination BC-7
Rose Hips
Chamomile Flowers
Slippery Elm Bark
Yarrow Herb
Capsicum Fruit
Golden Seal Root
Myrrh Gum
Peppermint Leaves
Sage Leaves
Lemon-grass Herb

Combination BC-8
Garlic Bulb
Rose Hips
Rosemary Leaves
Parsley Herb
Watercress Herb

Both **Combination BC-7** and **Combination BC-8** are used interchangably with colds and flus. Some people take them as preventatives.

Combination C-12
Lobelia Herb
Mullein Leaves

People tell me, "This unstuffs my head so I can sleep at night."

Combination BC-5
Bayberry Rootbark
Ginger Root
White Pine Bark
Capsicum Fruit
Cloves Flowers

This is Dr. Shook's famous composition powder. It seems to act as a catalyst to make other herbs work. My neighbor woke me one morning, aching in every bone with a stuffed head. She made a strong tea of this formula and drank a cup every hour. By the afternoon she was out shopping. I give this same combination to Summer when all her friends are falling over with School Flu. It seems to protect her.

Hot Tub

When you get desperate you can always try this. Herbalists say you'll often get results overnight.[15]

Run a hot tub of water. Toss in a handful of *Ginger* capsules and a handful of *Capsicum* capsules. (The capsules will melt.) These herbs can be loose if you have them in bulk. Hop in the tub and soak to your neck. Meanwhile, drink a hot cup of *Yarrow* tea. The idea is to sweat!

15. Advice from Dr. Christopher.

After 15 or 20 minutes, jump up, rinse yourself off and tear into bed. Tuck those covers right up around your chin and body. Hold still and sweat. You should run rivers of water. By morning the soaked bed will be dry and your cold almost gone.

Now, here's how **not** to do it.

How To Scratch Your Way To Health

Ludmilla the herbalist has another exciting story for us.

One night I got sick. Around midnight my husband, Isaac, woke me up.

"You need to get well. I'm going to run you that hot bath you're always talking about," he said.

"Oh no, Isaac, please," I begged. "I'm too sick."

Isaac swung his head and grinned. "That's when you're supposed to take the bath." I wondered if he was getting even.

I ended up in the tub. I sweated and soaked and suffered. "Please, Isaac, let me out of here," I pleaded.

"OK," he said. "But hurry up. I've got the bed turned down and you can't get cooled off."

I clambered out of the tub, ran a quick towel over myself and dashed for bed. I leaped in and Isaac quickly covered me. He tucked me in carefully like a little mummy.

"Now," he said wagging a finger at me. "Hold perfectly still. You can't let any cold air get in."

I held still and turned my mouth down in a sad-sack fashion. Nothing to do now but be quiet, not move...and sweat.

The sweating started. I ran rivers. I was wet and clammy. Then...what was this?

Prickling sensations. A little itch here. A bigger itch there. Mad itches were breaking out all over my tightly swaddled body. I wanted to scratch. I **had** to scratch. But I couldn't. If I moved, air would creep in and my healing would be ruined. Then various parts of my body began smarting with a stinging sensation. Stinging! Itching! Tears dribbled from my eyes. I felt rotten anyway and now to be afflicted with this. What was it? Aha! I remembered. I had forgotten to rinse off the *Ginger* and *Cayenne Pepper* (also known as *Capsicum*). Oh no! Taking a shower now was unthinkable. I'd have to do the bath bit all over again. My choice was clear. Suffer. I did. I was also well the next morning.

Hot Date

There's a man I know named Jerry. He says he hasn't been able to sweat for most of his life. But when he's taking those baths he sweats like a marathon runner. He loves it. Maybe it's not as fun as dinner and a show, but it's a different way to spend an evening.

Cough

A lady named Jeanne wants you to have her recipe for a cough:

Jeanne's Cough Recipe

One tablespoon *Honey*
One tablespoon *Lemon Juice*

PLUS

One capsule of *Slippery Elm Bark*
One capsule of *Ginger*

Mix it all together in hot water.

(I like to add some *Cayenne Pepper*. *Cayenne Pepper* and *Capsicum* are the same thing, but to me *"Cayenne Pepper"* describes it better.)

"Drink this," she says, "and you'll sleep all night."

I have found whenever I have a stubborn cough, *Siberian Ginseng* kicks the habit. The Chinese use it with any disease for fast healing. *Lobelia Extract* under the tongue will relax the cough reflex.

Flu And Cold Prevention

Some people take the *Composition Powder,* **Combination BC-5,** daily. Others take *Garlic* and/or **Combination BC-7.**

Combination BC-5	**Combination BC-7**
Bayberry Rootbark	*Rose Hips*
Ginger Root	*Chamomile Flowers*
White Pine Bark	*Slippery Elm Bark*
Capsicum Fruit	*Yarrow Herb*
Cloves Flowers	*Capsicum Fruit*
	Golden Seal Root
	Myrrh Gum
	Peppermint Leaves
	Sage Leaves
	Lemon-grass Herb

45

Hungry Sunday

My friends, Marlene and Adam, came to visit one Sunday. They'd been to one of those great brunches where you eat everything except the knobs off the bathroom doors. They'd had a marvelous time and loved the fancy food and variety. Unfortunately, it made them sick. After they'd rolled around in my chairs, moaned and complained for a while, I gave them hot *Peppermint* tea. It fixed them right up. They left, making plans to go back for brunch, the next Sunday.

Get Up And Golf

Another time, several women friends came by for an evening. Lacey promptly felt unwell and lay down on the floor. She groaned and rolled a bit. Several big tears sprang from her eyes. Sally and I peered down at her with sympathy.

"You want to take something for that?" I asked. "I have a combination of herbs that usually gives prompt relief for nausea, flu, vomiting, fever, diarrhea..."

"Oh shut up," Lacey said. I sat back, offended. Let her suffer. After she'd thrown up a few times she agreed to try some herbal tea. It worked so well she insisted we all suit up and go miniature golfing.

Lacey's Tea	
Combination BC-6 Ginger Root Capsicum Golden Seal Root Licorice Root	Useful with nausea, flu, vomiting, fever, diarrhea.

Lacey's combination is nice to have on hand. Haven't you noticed how you always get violently ill at 3 a.m. when everything's closed and no one feels like holding your hand?

Daughter Lives To See Mother Give Thanks

Pat's mother recently spent three days in the hospital and spent $1600. She had very loose green stools, stomach pain and couldn't hold anything down. The hospital couldn't help her at all. She came home to suffer and Pat took over. Pat told me, "I gave her herbs, of course. She made **me** take them first to prove they weren't poisonous! But, after one hour, Mom was on the way to recovery and she cooked...and

46

ate...Thanksgiving dinner the next day!"
She gave her:

Aloe Vera Juice
Thick *Slippery Elm* tea
Peppermint tea

After she felt better she started taking a special combination of *Enzymes* everyday so her food would digest.

Wanted: People With Bugs

If you're sick now and feel miserable, even have a fever, here's a comforting thought.

I got a call one morning from a lady named Melanie. "Oh Venus," she trilled. "I've had the most marvelous weekend. I was sick. I had a fever of 102°. I was so happy I was out of bed and literally jumping with joy. My husband thought I was hallucinating!"

I wondered aloud if she still was.

"Oh mercy no!" she replied. "My body feels so much lighter and less tense today after three days of fever. That fever burned up so many toxins and germs. I'm so thrilled. I read that some European doctors autopsied bodies of people who had died. They were full of infections. Their bodies hadn't had enough energy to cause a fever to **kill** those viruses and bacteria!"

She paused for breath and then said earnestly, "I don't see many people, Venus. I mainly stay at home, so, of course, I never get sick. Lucky for me, my husband must have brought something home from work. But now, I'm concerned. How am I going to get sick more often?" I listened disbelievingly as she stated, seriously, "I'm going to start getting out of the house more and mingle with sick people so I can get those bugs."

Stress—Nerves—Headaches

Herbs Abort Romance

Rose, about 50 years old, came to me with her sad tale. "My boyfriend, Harvey, got robbed the other night." She sat back and sucked her teeth. "They almost cleaned him out. The second night they came back and finished the job." She snorted indignantly. "All he has left are the clothes on his back. So I said to him, 'See Harvey. These kinds of things happen when you live alone. I should move in with you.' But he was very philosophical. 'No, no," he said to me, 'I'm just lucky I wasn't murdered. I'll be fine.' You know, Venus," Rose said with exasperation, "I've got this guy taking so many damn relaxing herbs he's not even hysterical enough to have me move in!"

Harvey's Nerve Helpers

| Herbal Calcium | **Combination B-1**
Comfrey Root
Alfalfa Herb
Oat Straw
Irish Moss Plant
Horsetail Herb
Lobelia Herb | **Single Herbs:**
Catnip
Chamomile
Valerian
Lobelia
Hawthorn
Licorice |
| Nerve Repair | **Combination B-16**
Black Cohosh Root
Capsicum Fruit
Valerian Root
Mistletoe Herb
Ginger Root
St. Johnswort Herb
Hops Flowers
Wood Betony Herb | |

All of these herbs and combinations are often used to relieve stress and rebuild the nervous system. Some are reputed to work on the adrenal glands.

Husband Looks Good Again

One lady complained, "For weeks I felt irritable and my husband's mere presence annoyed me. I took just one capsule of a **concentrated** form of the *Nerve Capsule* (see *Harvey's Helpers*) and peace came over me. I even found my husband looked good, again.

Ma Bell And Me

Lydia received a phone bill guaranteed to send her husband into shrieking fits. Before showing it to him she worked out a plan. At breakfast she slipped him six of Harvey's concentrated *Nerve Capsules* and three *Catnip*. She packed another four strong *Nerve Capsules* in his lunch with eight more *Catnip*. (He assumed he was taking his regular herbs.) Lydia called him at work to test him out. "How are you feeling, Honey...a little tired?...ummmm?" When he came home, his solicitous wife gave him another huge dose of the same herbs. Her report to me was. "...He was so mellow." Her eyes glittered and she grinned, "We had a **marvelous** night."

Headaches

Here's a general rule: "Clean 'em out and calm 'em down and most headaches go away." If a person is riddled with their own body poisons and wastes, of course they're going to feel it in some way. When I have a headache, I get my bowel moving. I also use the herbs for the nervous system. Migraine sufferers often stay on a daily clean-out and nerve building program and find relief.

For a headache that I can feel coming on, I often use:

Combination B-1 Comfrey Root Alfalfa Herb Oat Straw Irish Moss Plant Horsetail Herb Lobelia	A good relaxer with lots of natural calcium.

I take six capsules of **Combination B-1** at one time, along with six capsules of *Wood Betony* (historically used for pain in the head and face.)

Valerian Root: I swallow two or so capsules to get some instant relaxation.

Fenugreek and *Thyme:* Sometimes this works for heavy headache sufferers.

There's also an herbal oil on the market. It's an old Chinese remedy. Rubbed across the forehead and back of the neck, most common headaches leave in two minutes.

Some women suffer from headaches because of their hormonal cycle. Often too much estrogen in the woman's body causes the brain to swell producing headaches. Many women muscle test to see what herbs will alleviate the problem. Often it's *Siberian Ginseng* or *Sarsaparilla*.

Thundering Head

There's always the odd one. Two old ladies I know have an old man friend. In their words, "Ferdie's had miserable headaches for years...tsk, tsk...Terrible ones that start at the top of his head and go all the way down into his neck. He's found that by taking two capsules of the anti-cold formula, then two more later, his headaches will leave."

Ferdie's Fixer

Combination BC-5
Bayberry Rootbark
Ginger Root   Useful with headaches
White Pine Bark
Capsicum Fruit
Cloves Flowers

Man Sleeps Instead of Dies

Here's another of Ludmilla, the herbalist's, entertaining stories:

My husband, Isaac, practically fell out of bed one morning. His face was white, he was sweating and moaning. He had "terrible pain in my bowel." Then he was out of bed and onto the floor where he semi-crawled into a stink bug position. We couldn't figure out what his problem was, but he, true to form, wanted to go to the hospital. I, also true to form, wouldn't take him. We then had a big argument. He was demanding to be taken immediately to the hospital and I spent time stalling.

"Just hang on here a minute, Isaac," I said logically. I could well be logical. I wasn't the one in pain. "You've been under a lot of stress lately," I said. "Maybe it's affecting your bowel."

"So take me to the hospital!" he yelled.

"Now look, Isaac," I said. "We spend all our time teaching people how to take care of themselves and not run to the hospital for every minor thing."

"This is **not** minor," Isaac screamed.

"OK," I said. "I'll take you." I wrapped him in a blanket and trundled him into the back of my car. Then I whipped off down the road like a house on fire. To a chiropractor. What could Isaac do? He was incapacitated. The doctor gave him a barium X-ray which confirmed my suspicion. He had a spasm in his bowel.

Reaching into my pocket, I pulled out three *Valerian Root* and washed them down Isaac's throat. Within ten minutes he was asleep and out of pain.

You'd think Isaac would have been grateful, but, I don't think he was. I can't seem to leave my family alone. I have a constant urge to experiment with them and the herbs.

Tightening Summer's Screws

When I first started using herbs, Summer was about seven years old and very high strung. She would seem perfectly normal one moment and the next she was jerking, making faces and acting like her screws were loose.

One day my mother called, "I'm coming down for the day. Why don't you and Summer meet me for lunch?"

"Well sure," I said. "Good idea." After I hung up I got a clear mental picture of mother and me sitting over a leisurely lunch with Summer twitching, banging her plate, sliding under the table and hopping from foot to foot. Summer wasn't obnoxious and undiciplined, she simply couldn't hold still.

"Ummm," I thought. "I think I'll give her a little *Lobelia*. (*Lobelia* is a unique herb. It's called the "Thinking Herb" which means it works wherever there's a problem and it's very relaxing.)

Shortly before lunch time I called Summer to the kitchen. "Here Sum," I said. "Another herb for you." I gave her one *Lobelia*.

Lunch time came. Summer and Mom sat across from me. Mother and I were having a spirited conversation, uninterrupted by Summer. We talked and laughed, made plans and discussed our business affairs and family. Summer was perfectly still. Mother and I continued our animated discussion.

Then, very quietly, Summer spoke. "Mother?" She looked at me and I looked at her. Then I hunkered down and peered closer. She sure looked odd. Her eyes drooped and her mouth was slack. She was hunched disjointedly over her plate. "Mother," she said again, very slowly, "I don't know what's the matter with me..." She sunk a little lower in her seat. Like a slow record she continued, "I feel...so...funny..."

Oh my gosh! The *Lobelia*. I must have given her a bit too much. It wouldn't hurt her, but it sure struck me funny. I started laughing. She looked so strange. This little pale kid with her heavy lidded eyes tilted back and her mouth hanging open. "Oh Summer. Ha ha ha!" I managed. "I did it to you. I gave you too much *Lobelia*."

Summer managed to work up a very disgusted look. With authority in her slow voice she peered at me and pronounced, "Don't you...**ever**...do that...again."

I haven't.

51

Hyperactive Children

There's always *Lobelia*. Other mothers have found good results with consistent use with a lot of *Alfalfa, Calcium, Chamomile, Passion Flower* and the other nerve herbs. Some people think hyperactive children need toxins and metals removed from their blood. Following are some good blood purifiers:

Blood Purifiers		
Single Herbs:	*Combination C-1*	*Combination C-3*
Burdock	Yellow Dock Root	Licorice Root
Yellow Dock	Dandelion Root	Red Clover Tops
	Burdock Root	Sarsaparilla Root
	Licorice Root	Cascara Sagrada Bark
	Chaparral Herb	Oregon Grape Root
	Red Clover Tops	Chaparral Herb
	Barberry Rootbark	Burdock Root
	Cascara Sagrada Bark	Buckthorn Bark
	Yarrow Herb	Prickly Ash Bark
	Sarsaparilla Root	Peach Bark
		Stillingia Root

To Sleep Or Not To Sleep

One night, I couldn't sleep. Before going to bed I took two *Calcium* and three *Catnip*.

The next morning Summer said, "Those barking dogs kept me awake all night, and weren't you annoyed when the cats beat each other up in the hall and rolled down the stairs?"

I hadn't heard a thing.

Summer's Embarrassment

Here's another little trick I use with Summer. You know how girls like to have their friends over to stay the night? Then they giggle and talk and scream about boys until 3 or 4 in the morning. I don't like that. I like them to come over, have a good time and go to sleep. Early. I make sure they do. With bedtime, everyone gets several *Calcium* and a few capsules of an herbal *Sleep Combination*. Summer is horribly embarrassed and says, "Oh, Mother!" But they take them and they sleep.

Summer's Herbs

To Sleep	**Combination B-18**	**Single Herbs:**
	Valerian Root	*Calcium*
	Anise	*Passion Flower*
	Lobelia	*Lobelia Extract*
	Brigham Tea	
	Black Walnut	
	Licorice Root	
	Ginger Root	
Herbal Relaxer	**Combination B-15**	
	Valerian Root	
	Skullcap Herb	
	Hops Flowers	

Depression

Depression is so depressing. I vote to stamp it out. I've found these help:

Single Herbs:	**Combination B-10**	
Pau d'Arco	Capsicum Fruit	Instant
Kelp	Siberian Ginseng Root	Energy
A Trace Mineral Combination	Gotu Kola Herb	

Sometimes imbalanced hormones can be the cause. And sometimes cleaning the body can get rid of chronic depression.

How Ludmilla Faces Depression
(Another Exciting Ludmilla Story)

Pau d'Arco works for me. I'd been taking some for several weeks when I noticed the mood elevation. Isaac had lost his car keys. He was sure I'd put them somewhere. Like the good wife I was then, trained to accept guilt, I joined in the hunt, and bounded from room to room. I looked frantically for those keys. Isaac was yelling. He "had to be somewhere." He "was late." He "certainly would have put those keys" where he "could see them." I "was always putting" his "stuff away." Why couldn't I "leave his things alone?"

While trotting downstairs after a fruitless search of the hall closet, I suddenly thought, "Gee. Life is wonderful. I'm so happy." I broke out in a wide grin, joy oozing from the corners. I stopped short. "I shouldn't be happy. The keys are lost!" I laughed a little and said, "But, I am."

We eventually found the keys. Sticking out of the trunk lock on Isaac's car.

Hair, Skin And Nails

Most of us want to be beautiful. But what do we have in reality? Ladies, do you have a beautiful soul but your scalp shines through your hair under the street lights? Does your skin sag around your ankles and your rear end droop? Do your nails have a close relationship with the skin on your fingers? Does your face resemble a gravel pit with pockets? This goes for men, too. Uncountable people look at me morosely and plead, "What herbs can I take to grow hair...to grow long finger nails...to clear my skin and prevent wrinkles?"

Wrinkles

Lay your hand out flat. When you pinch the skin on the back of your knuckles does it remain standing up long after the rest of the congregation sits down? Does the skin on your neck and breasts look like a well-traveled bike path? You need *Potassium*. *Potassium* is found heavily in:

	Combination B-32	**Combination B-33**
Single Herbs:	Kelp	Dulse
Black Walnut Hulls	Dulse	Horsetail
AND	Watercress	Sage
	Wild Cabbage	Rosemary
	Horseradish	
	Horsetail	
	AND	

One lady began taking lots of *Comfrey* and swore that her wrinkles puffed out. I'd also drink lots of water and use a water based day and night cream. Does your lipstick run in tracks up to your nose and through your whiskers? There may be a *B Complex* and *Vitamin C* lack.

Other Skin Problems

White spots under the skin: These may come from clogged sebaceous glands. I'd use a good scrub puff and *Blood purifiers.*
White spots on the skin: Look to the liver and kidneys.

Warts

I had a stubborn wart for years on my chest. When I increased my organic *Vitamin A* to 100,000 IU daily, for a month or two, it and another wart, left. Some herbalists use *Black Walnut, Pau d'Arco, Zinc* and *Chaparral.* Warts are stubborn. Results can take months. If nothing else works, call my father. He'll run a black thread over your wart, then tell you to close your eyes. He will then race outside and bury the thread. When the thread rots the wart will be gone. Works every time.

Hair And Nails... Or Burr Headed Margie

Margie came to see me practically in tears. She was losing more hair than her husband. In desperation she'd had her hair fried with a permanent to add "body." She looked like she was wearing a cap of corkscrews.

After three months on an herbal program, she was back and crowing, "Look! Look!" Enthusiastically she leaned toward me. I almost collapsed with laughter. She had grown a short set of new hair that stood at attention through the tattered remains. She looked like a burr. And she loved it. Eventually the burr grew out and she had a full head of hair. She also acquired a long hard set of nails. Many men also use Margie's program with good results.

Margie's Hair

Horsetail: This is a plant, not a real horse's tail.
Jojoba Oil: Rubbed on the scalp at night.
A Good Herbal Shampoo

| Herbal Calcium | **Combination B-1**
Comfrey Root
Alfalfa Herb
Oat Straw
Irish Moss Plant
Horsetail Herb
Lobelia Herb

AND | **Combination B-33**
Dulse
Horsetail
Sage
Rosemary | Hair, Skin and Nails |

Sage has a reputation for restoring color to hair and *Yarrow* supposedly makes hair curly. For thicker hair, some people mix *Aloe Vera Jell* and *Jojoba Oil* together and rub it through their hair at night. (No, they don't have any love life, that's why they're using this desperate method.) In the morning they shampoo. They tell me this process gives their hair a thicker feel and appearance.

For desperate people, especially men, here's another option.

The Bald-Headed Fellow With Furry Cheeks

There's a combination of herbs[16] used as a poultice, usually for bones, joints, ligaments and cartilage repair. Someone told Ludmilla's husband Isaac that it would grow hair on his head. That's all it took. Here's Ludmilla's story:

"The next evening I soaked and simmered up a batch of *Guaranteed* **(possibly)** *Hair Restorer.* When I finished, I left Isaac to his own devices. Tell me what you would think if you heard some clattering and singing in the kitchen, went to investigate and found your husband stark naked except for his shoes and socks. Not only was Isaac in that condition, but he had his back to me at the kitchen sink. His furry cheeks quivered with each aria. Around his waist was an ace bandage with an odd lump at back and center. He also wore a plastic vegetable bag over his head and under that was another ace bandage wound over his head and under his chin. This wrapping sported a lump on the crown. He'd been busy. With full confidence, he'd whipped together two poultices. One to grow hair on his head and the other to repair the disc in his back. It might have worked, who knows, but it was the only time he tried it.

The Miracle Hair Restorer
(Possibly)

Combination B-30
White Oak Bark
Comfrey Root
Mullein Leaves
Black Walnut Leaves
Marshmallow
Queen of the Meadow
Wormwood Herb
Lobelia
Skullcap

---

16. Advice from Dr. Christopher.

Sin Problems

Wandering Herpes

On one of my lecture tours I was discussing a woman's herpes. A wispy little old man raised his hand, "Where were those herpes?" My answer was, "Anywhere you want them to be."

They're all related. Mouth herpes, vaginal herpes, cold sores or canker sores. And they're all miserably uncomfortable. If you have them lurking in your system, stress seems to bring them out to devil you further.

Alice's Daughter

Alice told me, "My daughter had suffered for years with cold sores. I told her what to do, herbally. She took a *Blood Purifying Combination*[17], an *Herbal Nerve Combination*[18] and *Black Walnut Hulls*. She put the liquid *Black Walnut* right on the sores and said the pain left immediately. She also took the *Black Walnut* internally. She said the cold sores left in seven days. She wouldn't listen to anything I told her before, and now, suddenly, she thinks I'm smart! I told her not to test this piece of advice, but that the same program is used with excellent results, by genital herpes sufferers.

More Herpes

Jeri says, "This is the first summer I haven't had cold sores. I give full credit to the bowel cleansers."

Jan was ecstatic, "I got rid of mouth herpes in one day! I used *Pau d'Arco*."

17. See Appendix I
18. See Appendix I

57

Skin Problems

Woman Almost Itches To Death

Sybil was getting a divorce. "I was so nervous that I broke out in huge welts all over my body. Then I got this eczema stuff on my hands, behind my ears, on my eyelids and in my eyebrows. I was really fetching. I rubbed that *Chinese Herbal Oil* on the welts which stopped the itching. Then I took an *Herbal Nervine Combination* plus a *Combination of Herbs* for hair, skin and nails. In 24 hours there was a huge improvement.

Itchy Blood And Bodies

Nita came into my shop laughing. "Venus," she grinned. "My Dad has been taking herbs and doing so well. But, he got a rash and thought he'd better see a doctor. I said, 'Dad. The doctor is just going to look you over, say, "ummm" and give you a prescription for cortisone and that's it. It'll cost you 50 bucks, too.' " Nita laughed out loud. "It happened just that way. As the doctor wrote out the prescription, my Dad started laughing. He explained to the doctor that his daughter had told him what he would say and do. This ticked off the doctor who brought in another doctor for a second opinion. That doctor said the same thing. My dad said, 'Forget it. I'm going back on my daughter's herbs. I feel fabulous with them!' "

Most of the time when a person has a rash, boils or other skin conditions, including acne, something is trying to get out of the body. Does it make sense to try and push it back in? Whenever I get a skin weirdness I start taking:

A *Blood Purifier*

OR

Single blood purifiers like *Yellow Dock, Burdock* or *Aloe Vera Juice.*

The skin problem may get worse at first, as everyone tries to jump ship, but I expect that.

Libby's Poison Oak

This is a sorry tale. Libby's husband went on a hike. A few days later

Libby's husband gave her poison oak in a very private place. Libby was furious; he hadn't bothered to tell her he had it **there**.

Libby took lots of *Yellow Dock* and the poison oak was gone in several days. Her husband opted for cortisone shots. Two weeks later he was still a scratching celibate.

Serves him right.

Acne

Rotten skin can be caused by several things.

1. Toxic blood. (I'd use *Blood Purifiers.*[19])

2. Toxic bowel. (There's always the *Comfrey-Pepsin Cleanse.*)

3. Nerves and stress. (Consider the *Nervines.*[20])

4. Bacteria. (If antibiotics clear up the skin, consider taking *Garlic* capsules. For best results, the kind that stink.)

5. Hormone imbalance. (I'd do muscle testing with various hormone acting herbs. See Combinations in Appendix I.)

Adolescent boys and young men with acne seem to clear up remarkably well with *Sarsaparilla* and *Siberian Ginseng* in combination. These herbs balance male hormones. You **do** know the other side effect don't you? They're favorites of older men for their **sexy** side effects. I got a good laugh the other day. I know a very sweet, kind, demure, religious lady. She's the type that's so cool, butter wouldn't melt on her body. She pursed up her lips a little bit and told me, "My Harold (age 11) had the worst skin. But, I'm giving him just tons of *Sarsaparilla* and *Siberian Ginseng.*"

"My gawd lady," I thought. "Do you know what you've **done** to little Harold?"

"You know," she continued, "his skin's so much better...and his out look, well, my, his outlook seems so much different...somehow..."

(*Sarsaparilla* and *Siberian Ginseng* in moderation are perfectly OK.)

19. See Appendix I
20. See Appendix I

Bones, Joints, Ligaments, Cartilage

The natural use for the *Miracle* **(possibly)** *Hair Restorer* is for bones, joints, tissue, ligaments and cartilage.

Elizabeth Delivers

Elizabeth, a mail-lady, delivered a packet of mail to an old man on her route. He was lonesome and said, "Dearie, come in and see my cat," She tried, fell through his door and fractured her knee cap. Later, while in a cast, she rolled down a driveway and damaged her other knee. She brewed up some of our *Miracle Poultice,* slapped it on and kept it there until midnight when she said the swelling left. The next day she had no bruises. She began taking several other formulas internally for bone repair along with straight *Comfrey.* Later when her cast was removed, her doctor was stupified. He found no *Calcium* buildup and said no one could ever look at her X-rays and know she'd broken the knee.

Elizabeth's Repair Job

Combination B-30
White Oak Bark
Comfrey Root
Mullein Leaves
Black Walnut Leaves
Marshmallow
Queen of the Meadow
Wormwood Herb
Lobelia
Skullcap

AND

Combination B-29
Comfrey Root
Golden Seal Root
Slippery Elm Bark
Aloe Leaves (Resin)

Single Herbs:
Comfrey

AND

Combination B-31
Comfrey
Dandelion
Ginseng
Wood Betony

Single Herbs:
Comfrey

All of these are used for bone, joint, tissue, ligament, and cartilage repair.

Ears And Eyes
Ears That Kick, Scratch and Pain

Lucy leaned toward her husband one night and whispered frantically, "Dick, Dick listen! Do you hear mites in my ears?" She told me later she could hear something in there kicking and scratching. She figured she'd gotten ear mites from her new kitten. Several days of putting liquid herbal extract in her ears and the commotion cooled down and left.

A man used this same extract for ear ringing and found instead that his hearing vastly improved.

There are many mothers who will be delighted to know Susan's formula for children's ear infections. She used the same herbal extract mentioned above. She squirts it down their throats and into their ears, then pops another herbal remedy into their screaming mouths. She says it works. She should know. Every winter she used to have five children with ear infections.

Susan's Formula For Ear Infections

Combination C-13
Chickweed
Black Cohosh
Goldenseal Root
Lobelia
Skullcap
Brigham Tea
Licorice Root

(This is an extract.) Susan puts this liquid combination in her children's ears when they have ear aches or infections.

Combination C-10
Echinacea Root
Golden Seal Root
Yarrow Flowers
Capsicum Fruit

Susan gives this internally for infection.

My daughter, Summer, has her own remedy for ear infections. We spent a lot of time using herbs that work for others: *Lobelia Extract* is historically used in the ears for pain. *Capsicum Extract* is rubbed around the ear to bring circulation to that area. *Garlic Oil* is put in the ears by many who have ear infections.

However, Summer found that squirting cold *Aloe Vera Juice* in her ears with an eye dropper worked best. Once when Summer was wild with pain and **nothing** helped, I cut an onion in half and baked it. Summer held half close to the painful ear. She said it pulled the pain out.

61

The Green Eyed Lady

The phone rang. I lunged for it and the light. It was 4 a.m. My heart beat frantically. Who'd been killed on the road? "Hello," I said, hoping my wits would sharpen.

"Oh God!" yelled a woman.

"No," I said, "You've got the wrong number."

The lady continued. "Is this Venus? Venus, I'm in Michigan."

(Yes, I thought and I'm in California, three hours behind you.)

"I've got long green runners coming out of my eyes. They run out and down my cheeks every ten minutes. Can you imagine how embarrassing that is? People look at me and say 'Yowee, there are strings coming out of your eyes!' I'm taking six herbal capsules a day and making a strong tea out of another three capsules and straining it just like I'm supposed to. I'm also rinsing my eyes three to five times a day and look what it's doing." The nameless woman gave a lingering wail.

This is a hard way to wake up. However, I valiantly sat up, faced the blackness outside my windows and congratulated her.

"This is wonderful. I'm so happy for you." (Remember my axiom? Better **out** than **in**!) I continued, "Many people find their eyes sticking shut, pass mucus and gritty stuff, think their eye sight is getting worse, get red eyes and other disturbing phenomena. Usually these are good signs; the eyes are cleansing. After six months or so, many people say their glaucoma, or cataracts have improved or disappeared. Others say they regain their former eyesight. I'm not saying you will, but many do. OK?"

"Oh yeah?" the lady asked. "Hey. I'm lucky then, right? I'm getting some action. Well thanks. I'll call again."

Lucky Steve

An older fellow named Steve began taking the *Eye Formula* for cataracts. After about four months he announced that he'd been deaf in one ear for 36 years, but that morning his hearing had returned. (Herbs have interesting side effects.) Steve later added *Chickweed* for the ear problem.

"My Grandad"

A friend reported this one to me: "My grandad is thrilled. He used to have, according to him, 'weekly glaucoma attacks.' Since he started the *Eye Formula* plus extra *Eyebright,* he's had only one small attack. I've seen yellowish, greenish junk come out of his eyes. He says they even itch and tear. But, you know what's funny? He had trouble mixing the tea. You know how you boil water, pour it in a tea cup and then open three capsules and pour the herbs in the cup? Put a saucer on top and let it sit 20 minutes and then strain it? Well. He was throwing them in, capsule and all! Can you imagine trying to rinse your eyes with that mixture?"

Grandad's Eye Mix

OR

Combination BC-14
Golden Seal Root
Bayberry Rootbark
Eyebright Herb

Single Herbs:
Eyebright

Combination BC-15
Golden Seal Root
Bayberry Rootbark
Eyebright Herb
Red Raspberry Leaves
Capsicum Fruit

Many sissies start with the first formula because it's milder. They work up to the stronger. If they find it burns their eyes too badly they just dilute the mixture. The burning sensation won't hurt the eyes, but may leave them red.

Laughing Linda

Linda D. is spending a lot of time laughing because her mother, Jean, used to spend a lot of time packaging up and returning all the herbs Linda forced on her. "Thank you very much dear, but I don't need these and they wouldn't work, anyway."

Then, disaster struck. Jean's doctor told her she was going blind. "No hope. Face up to it. Accept it." She had a strange malady. Cysts in her eyes with tremendous pain and deterioration of the eyeballs.

Linda went into action. She loaded her mother's arms with herbs and her desperate mother took them. After about six months of steady use the cysts left. So did the pain. Jean's eyes came to life. No more fears of blindness.

Just last week Linda's mother called and admonished her, insisting that Linda take this herb and another, explaining in detail why she should. Linda got a big laugh out of it, as she had been the original pusher in the family.

Jean's Eye Reversal

Single Herbs:
Vitamin A

Black Walnut Hulls

High in *Potassium*. (It's suspected that people with cysts, tumors, warts and moles have a *Potassium* lack.)

Combination B-32
Kelp
Dulse
Watercress
Wild Cabbage
Horseradish
Horsetail

This is high in *Potassium*.

Combination BC-14
Golden Seal Root
Bayberry Rootbark
Eyebright Herb

The combinations for eyes.

OR

Combination BC-15
Golden Seal Root
Bayberry Rootbark
Eyebright Herb
Red Raspberry Leaves
Capsicum Fruit

PLUS

A good bowel cleanse.

Many people with cataracts find the Eye Formulas helpful.

Brain

Middy's Dilemma

Jack's grandmother, Middy, is senile. Jack told me, "Once I kissed her 'hello.' She turned to my mother, clearly annoyed, and said, 'Who **was** that man?' " She's so senile, that with a beatific smile she will wander to the roadside and start taking off her clothes. She's a dear lady and everyone loves her, but it's hard to communicate. Jack said one day he and his wife gifted Middy's daughter, (his mother), with a bottle of *Gotu Kola*. His instructions, "Mom, just try this with Grandma. It's worked with lots of people who say it reverses senility, prevents it and brings back the memory."

Mom gave it to Middy, daily. She called after about three weeks to say, "I can really see a difference, Jack." Jack was delighted. "As soon as you need another bottle, let me know, Mom."

Weeks went by, then months, with no call from Mom. Finally, Jack called her. "What's happening with Middy? Why haven't you called for *Gotu Kola*?" There was a sigh at the other end of the line. "I had to stop giving it to her. Your step-father said it worked too well." There was a pause. "He said she was remembering things best left forgotten."

Average Joes

Mary Jane had, in her words, "three, rather average, little boys. Until I started giving them *Gotu Kola*. Then I got a phone call from their school. They want to put the kids in a gifted program. Suddenly the teachers are making a flap over their cleverness! The little yo-yos have recently sprouted the ear marks of genius."

Stuttering Stan

Stan, 9 years old, had stuttered all his life. Three months ago his mother whipped up her own version of an herbal anti-stuttering regime and today he's stutter free.

Stuttering Stan's Regime

Single Herbs:

Gotu Kola   For the brain.

Continued...

Bayberry	(Historically used for mucus and obstructions in the head area.)
Hops	A relaxant

Combination B-16		**Combination B-17**
Black Cohosh Root		*Black Cohosh Root*
Capsicum Fruit		*Capsicum Fruit*
Valerian Root	OR	*Valerian Root*
Mistletoe Herb		*Mistletoe Herb*
Ginger Root		*Lady's Slipper Root*
St. Johnswort Herb		*Lobelia Herb*
Hops Flowers		*Skullcap Herb*
Wood Betony Herb		*Hops Flowers*
		Wood Betony Herb

Both **Combination B-16** and **Combination B-17** are used for nerve repair.

Seizures

Many people have reported improvement or relief of symptoms with:
Gotu Kola
Blessed Thistle: Reportedly gets oxygen to the brain and heart area.

Betty mentioned she'd been beaten by her ex-husband. He'd punched her in the head and ever since she'd felt "A pressure and something growing in there. It scares me." She took *Bayberry* and the feeling left.

Extrasensory Perception

Different people have told me that *Siberian Ginseng* seems to activate their ESP.

Phobias and Fears

One of my brothers won't touch Jack-in-the-Box door handles or escalator rails. He has a germ phobia. Last Thanksgiving one of my sister-in-laws and I chased him all over the house trying to kiss him. He was a shrieking bundle of panic. Kissing has germs.

Most people I know have some fear or phobia they keep tucked away. They're afraid and embarrassed to voice it. One lady was even tormented by evil voices in her head. The same herb seems helpful for all of them:

Black Walnut Hulls.

It's also reputed to be excellent if you're struck by lightening, or otherwise electrified.

PART IV

Herbs Traditionally Used For Those Interesting Problems Having To Do With:

Sex

Women

Babies

"Few things are more important to a community than the health of its women."

T.W. Higginson

Sex

Meatloaf For Dinner Brings Love In The Night

An herbalist friend told me this one: A woman came to see her saying, "You've got to help me. My husband just isn't interested in me anymore. You must have something to stimulate desire."

My friend suggested an *Herbal Combination* to strengthen and repair all the sexual organs, plus *Siberian Ginseng* and *Sarsaparilla*. Her client was delighted.

"But, don't tell my husband," she begged. "I'm not going to tell him about this. I'm going to slip the herbs into his meatloaf. And I'm going to give him more capsules and tell him they're for his asthma! Good idea, huh?"

"Well," the herbalist said. "You know your husband."

A month or so went by. Apparently the wife was quite enthusiastic about that asthma treatment because the husband came in to see the herbalist. He sunk down into a chair and mopped his face, the picture of desperation.

"Lady," he breathed, "You've got to help me. All I can think about is sex!"

When I tell this story on lecture tours, a surprising number of women admit to slipping herbs into their husband's meals. And...the favorite hiding place is **meatloaf!**

Christmas Comes Early

My phone rang. "Hey Venus, this is Rachel down in San Diego. You know? Remember the stuff I got for that real old guy in my trailer park?" There was an embarrassed pause. "You know, his life wasn't worth living anymore? He was thinking of dying? You said if it was you, you'd try a combination of herbs for sex, plus *Siberian Ginseng* and *Sarsaparilla*, and that should give him something new to think about? Remember?"

"Oh, sure," I said.

"Well," Rachel gave a funny giggle. "He was just over here to see me. He says that stuff has changed his life. He's now got so many girlfriends he can't handle them all, but he's been **trying**. He says that stuff really works. He's so excited he's acting like a kid with a new toy!! Ha! Ha! Ha! He says it's too much for him, he's going to have to lay low for a while. And, Venus, what's so surprising is, all his life he was such a

moderate man, never drank, smoked or chased women!"

The Meatloaf Cure

Single Herbs:
Siberian Ginseng
Sarsaparilla

Combination B-23
Siberian Ginseng Root
Echinacea Root
Saw Palmetto Berries
Gotu Kola Herb
Damiana Leaves
Sarsaparilla Root
Periwinkle Herb
Garlic Bulb
Capsicum Fruit
Chickweed Herb

To Tone Tony Down

On the flip side...

Here's something I accidentally did to my father. I've never told him, so reading this should be a fun surprise for him.

Dad likes to worry. Worrying, to him, is an art form. But sometimes he overdoes it and can't function. During one of these spells I broke my self-imposed rule of "don't try to help Dad, he'd rather suffer" and gave him a bottle of *Skullcap. Skullcap* is a wonderful herb. It historically calms and repairs the nervous system; works on the medulla (the base of the brain where all automatic functions like heart beat and breathing originate) and repairs the spinal cord. I thought it would be just the ticket. However, I hadn't reckoned on my father. If directions say take six capsules, Daddy will figure he's different and take 12. That must be what happened, because within a month he had hot-footed, lickety-slickety down to my herb shop.

"Ah-um," he looked at me and cleared his throat. "Your mother and I have a problem. Something's not working right." I got the drift. He continued, "You must have something for **that** with all these damned herbs. Hell, this never happened to me before." He looked woe-begone, stricken and on the verge of middle-age panic. With a nervous jerk he threw up his hands. "Hell, I'm getting old!" His jowls sagged with despondency. His eyes blurred.

"Come on, Daddy," I soothed. "It's probably just a temporary lapse. You've been under a lot of stress. I've got some herbs that will fix you right up!"

My father's eyes flickered with hope. The man who didn't believe in herbs was now ready and willing to be convinced of their powers. He was hoping hard.

Shortly, he left with his little package clutched tightly to his chest. As soon as he was out the door I whipped open my herb book. I had a nagging suspicion that I might be involved in my father's dilemma. I flipped quickly to *Skullcap* and ran my finger down the list of attributes. There it was! I stopped breathing for a moment and looked stupid. *Skullcap:* **Used to suppress undue sexual desire.**

"Oh boy," I whispered. "I'll never tell 'im. If he knew what I did to him, he'd never take herbs again."

I chalked that little oversight to experience and went on with my life. Sorry Dad.

There's another herb that traditionally tones you down if too much is used. It's *Hops.* You know, of course, that beer is made from *Hops.* I get such a kick out of TV beer commercials. All these masculine-looking men lifting their foaming mugs, grinning and pounding their chests with old-boy-macho brotherhood. Never dreaming what they're drinking.

To Ex-Sex

Single Herbs:
Skullcap
Hops

I wonder how many meatloaves are being cooked tonight?...Hey, serve it with beer.

The Opposite Sex
Let's Hear It For A Good Time

More often, men want something to perk up their wives. One such man was Billie-Bob. One day he blew into my office and demanded that I give him something for his wife.

"There's got to be something for Frieda," he bellowed. "She's got no interest in sex."

He took home some herbs and my fervent expressions of good luck.

A month or two later, Frieda called. "Hi," she trilled. "It's working." I was delighted. "Oh, I dunno," she sang. "I dunno if Billie-Bob's too happy about it. Suddenly, I'm looking at all the men on the street. There's a fascinating bunch out there."

A month or so after that, gossip dribbled back to me. Frieda had taken a lover. From there she moved out on Billie-Bob and the last I heard, was living the good life.

Billie-Bob should have taken some of his own medicine.

Frieda's Special

Combination B-23
Siberian Ginseng Root
Echinacea Root
Saw Palmetto Berries
Gotu Kola Herb
Damiana Leaves
Sarsaparilla Root
Periwinkle Herb
Garlic Bulb
Capsicum Fruit
Chickweed Herb

AND

Single Herbs:
Damiana

Another lady came to me with an earnest request. "I want some herbs to rev up my husband...and I want some for my lover, too."

Why not? Who am I to judge?

Herbs For Women's Problems

These herbs are good for women and often contain natural, estrogen-like, qualities:

Herb	Historical Uses
Red Raspberry	Good for women generally.
Blessed Thistle	Female problems.
Damiana	For relief of hot flashes and to make one feel sexy.
Black Cohosh	A natural estrogen quality.
Dong Quoi	Similar to *Black Cohosh*.
Saw Palmetto	For breast enlargement.

A hormone balancer for both sexes.

Combination B-23
Siberian Ginseng Root
Echinacea Root
Saw Palmetto Berries
Gotu Kola Herb
Damiana Leaves
Sarsaparilla Root
Periwinkle Herb
Garlic Bulb
Capsicum Fruit
Chickweed Herb

Combination B-5
Golden Seal Root
Red Raspberry Leaves
Black Cohosh Root
Queen of the Meadow Herb
Marshmallow Root
Blessed Thistle Herb
Lobelia Herb
Capsicum Fruit
Ginger Root

A female hormone balancer.

A female hormone balancer used by women who have a tendency to miscarry, or by those who can't take estrogen.

Combination B-6
Golden Seal Root
Capsicum Fruit
False Unicorn Root
Ginger Root
Uva Ursi Leaves
Cramp Bark
Squaw Vine Herb
Blessed Thistle Herb
Red Raspberry Leaves

Continued...

	Combination B-7
	Black Cohosh Root
	Licorice Root
A male and female	False Unicorn Root
blend.	Siberian Ginseng Root
	Sarsaparilla Root
	Squaw Vine Herb
	Blessed Thistle Herb

Sarsaparilla and *Ginseng* contain the hormones *Progesterone* and *Testosterone*. Some women need these hormones.

Combination B-19	**Combination B-20**
Kelp Plant	Irish Moss Plant
Irish Moss Plant	Kelp Plant
Parsley Plant	Black Walnut Hulls
Capsicum Fruit	Parsley Herb
	Watercress Herb
	Sarsaparilla Root
	Iceland Moss Plant

Combination B-19 and **Combination B-20** may be helpful. They balance out the thyroid and entire glandular system.

Kathie is a lady who's tested these herbs on herself. When she takes the *Sarsaparilla* and *Ginseng,* she says she becomes very ambitious and aggressive. She gets a lot done and her business prospers. When she takes the estrogen-like female herbs, she finds herself close to her toasty fireplace, humming, stitching ruffles on curtains and tatting doilies. "Disgusting," she says. "I turn into a model housewife."

Women's Big Problems

Research shows there can be prevention and even reversal of uterine fibroids, cysts, breast soreness, cystic breasts, breast tumors, uterine hemorrhaging, endometriosis and even breast cancers. These problems are often related and can come from estrogen not being broken down correctly in the liver of some women. This research comes from Dr. Carlton Fredericks.[21] According to him, daily doses of certain vitamins and minerals can prevent and often reverse the conditions mentioned above.

This is my daily program for hormone problems based on my interpretation of Dr. Frederick's research:

21. *Winning The Fight Against Breast Cancer,* Dr. Carlton Fredericks

Hormone Problems

Vitamin E: 400-1200 units a day

Vitamin A: 25,000 units. 1-2 a day

Vitamin B Complex: 2-6 a day

Vitamin C: Time release—1000 milligrams 3 times a day

Kelp: For *Iodine.* 4-6 capsules per day

Selenium: Found in *Kelp* and *Garlic*

Garlic: Studies I've read about seem to show garlic can prevent tumors and cancers. 1-2 capsules per day

Black Walnut: The same as Garlic, plus used for cysts and warts. 4 capsules a day

Food Enzymes: I take 2 each meal to make sure my herb and vitamin program is being absorbed.

I also keep my **bowel clean**! Right now, it's the *Comfrey-Pepsin Cleanse.*

At the present time I am taking one of the following combinations for my liver. (I'll work on my liver for three or four months, then switch to another area that I feel needs some work.)

Liver

Combination BC-3
Red Beet Root
Dandelion Root
Parsley Herb
Horsetail (Shavegrass) Herb
Liverwort Herb
Birch Leaves
Lobelia Herbs
Blessed Thistle Herb
Angelica Root
Chamomile Flowers
Gentian Root
Golden Rod Herb

OR

Combination BC-4
 Barberry Root Bark
Ginger Root
Cramp Bark
Fennel Seeds
Peppermint Leaves
Wild Yam Root
Catnip Herb

These two products are also traditionally used to clean, flush and repair the liver.

Single Herbs:
 Chlorophyll
A loe Vera Juice

By following this program, many of my hormone-related symptoms have disappeared.

Endometriosis

One woman took the above program for quite a while plus, *Bayberry*, and these combinations:

Traditionally used as a deep-cell cleanser.	**Combination C-4** Gentian Root Echinacea Root Irish Moss Plant Black Walnut Hulls Golden Seal Root Barberry Rootbark Comfrey Root Dandelion Root Fenugreek Seeds St. Johnswort Herb Mandrake Root Chickweed Herb Safflower Flowers Catnip Herb Myrhh Gum Cyani (Cornflower) Flower Yellow Dock Root
A hormone balancer.	**Combination B-5** Golden Seal Root Blessed Thistle Herb Red Raspberry Leaves Lobelia Herb Black Cohosh Root Capsicum Fruit Queen of the Meadow Herb Ginger Root Marshmallow Root
Used traditionally as a vaginal suppository.	**Combination BC-21** Squawvine Chickweed Slippery Elm Comfrey Yellow Dock Golden Seal Root Mullein Marshmallow

My Cousin, Laura

Since I've made my father famous, I might as well do it for my cousin Laura. I was visiting with her one day when I casually said, "How are you, Laura?"

She took my question seriously and told me. Apparently she was having some female problems and couldn't find any relief.

You know me. I hopped right in and said, "Well, hey, Laura, why don't you try a vaginal bolus? That's like a suppository." Laura looked at me. Her lips crinkled with distaste. I forged ahead. "There's a combination of herbs formulated by Dr. Christopher. He says it's for cysts, tumors, polyps, cancers, infections...anything in the female area that shouldn't be there. It draws and pulls toxins and congestions even from the bowel, kidneys and bladder..."

"Oh yeah?" Laura looked interested.

"Yep," I continued. "Now listen to me carefully. Here's how women use it. They mix the powdered herbs with cocoa butter or vegetable glycerine, to a doughy consistency. Then they roll it into a tube the shape, length and width of the middle finger. You got that? Laura?"

"Sure," Laura nodded.

"OK," I went on. "Then they put these herb tubes in the refrigerator and let them harden. Next they take one out and grease it with olive oil...And," I said with emphasis, "they operate. They insert it up their vagina at bedtime. You got that?"

"Sure," was Laura's answer.

I hurried on, "They leave it in overnight and douche with *Yellow Dock* tea the next morning. A new suppository is put in each night, followed with a *Yellow Dock* tea douche the next morning, for six weeks to six months, however long it takes. I've seen dramatic results." I stopped, out of breath and expectant. "What do you think?" I asked.

Laura shrugged, "I'll try it."

Laura's herbs were mailed the next day.

A month or so later there was a big family gathering. I spotted Laura and ran up to her with a grin. I knew she'd be glad to see me and maybe I'd even get a nice thank you kiss.

"Hey, Laura!" I grabbed her hand. "How'd that stuff work?"

"**You**!" Laura snapped. "I'm really upset with you!"

"Me?" I quavered in a squeaky voice. "Why? Aren't you better?"

"No!" Laura hissed. "I'm worse! I mixed that stuff up just like you said. I rolled it into a finger shape. I hardened it in the refrigerator and then I greased it. But, I'll tell you," she snorted, "everytime I tried to shove that thing down my throat, I almost choked!!"

Laura's Special

Combination BC-21
Squawvine
Chickweed
Slippery Elm   Vaginal bolus
Comfrey
Yellow Dock
Golden Seal Root
Mullein
Marshmallow

You Swallowed What?

To digress a bit, I think this sort of thing runs in the family.

My father was seeing an oriental acupuncturist. Dr. Tong suggested some herbs, along with the needle treatments.

Of course, my Dad said, "Hot do! That's a good idea." (A doctor suggested herbs, not his daughter.)

He was given a 12-piece set of red silk boxes. When he got home, he and my mother opened one. There sat a waxy, gray ball the size of a small chicken egg.

"Oooh," my father said with awe.

My mother was more practical. "How are you going to get that thing down?"

Daddy rounded his eyes and looked horrified at the thought. How the heck **was** he going to get that swallowed? But Dr. Tong had given it to him and, by golly, Dr. Tong expected him to take it.

Mother told me later that it was quite an interesting afternoon. Dad would put that "egg" in his mouth, look at her and swallow. Still there. They tried water. Juice. Coffee. Tea. Dad got it stuck a few times and almost lost his lunch. At last, a glass of wine and a pickle pusher sent it squeezing down my father's throat. But alas! There it stayed.

As mom said, "Your father got it down all right, but there it sat, big as a golf ball and just a bit below his Adam's Apple. I had to toss him back in his chair and massage that thing the rest of the way down! It took 20 minutes."

...Maybe **that** was a suppository?

Cramps And Periods

Beverly used to have cramps so bad that three days out of every month she was sedated. Knocked out cold. She had a standing prescription for pain killers at the drug store. The cramps so up-ended her that the only job she could hold was as a waitress. It was understood by every employer that three days out of every month, Beverly would be absent. She'd been from doctor to doctor with no relief. The last doctor she'd seen had told her he had the answer. "I'll operate. I'll cut all the nerves to your uterus. You'll never feel a thing, again."

Two months on herbs and Bev called me. "It's amazing. By my second period all I felt was a slight twinge and my period started."

It's remained that way.

Bev's Cramp Cutter

A *Calcium* and
Silicon combination.
A traditional
relaxant.

Combination B-1
Comfrey Root
Alfalfa Herb
Oat Straw
Irish Moss Plant
Horsetail Herb
Lobelia Herb

Continued...

```
Combination B-5
Golden Seal Root
Red Raspberry Leaves
Black Cohosh Root              A traditional
Queen of the Meadow Herb       hormone balancer.
Marshmallow Root
Blessed Thistle Herb
Lobelia Herb
Capsicum Fruit
Ginger Root
```

Cramps Right Now!

I take:

One *Black Cohosh*

OR

Three or four *Calcium* capsules

OR

One *Ginger*

A lady named Mary had cramps so bad they sometimes sent her to the hospital. She found relief with this combination:

```
Combination B-15
Valerian Root           Another traditional
Skullcap Herb           relaxant.
Hops Flowers
```

Mary took five to six capsules at a time.

Hormone Balance Or Replacement

When women go off the Pill, go through menopause, have a hysterectomy, are under stress or even just seem normal, they sometimes go into a hormonal tailspin. We may sweat, freeze, bleed too much or not enough, feel depressed, cry, tire easily, crave sweets, feel sexy or frigid, scream and yell, batter our husbands and more. Once, right before my mother's period, I saw her sit down and eat an entire three pound box of chocolates. I remembered it, years later, when right before some of my periods, I would have killed for a candy bar. I used to bribe my ex-husband's kids to hop on their bikes late at night and hustle to the 7-11 for candy. That weirdness could strike night or day.

Balancing hormones isn't easy. I noticed I could take a straight herb or a combination and it would work wonderfully well. And the next day it didn't. Or, the next week or month, my symptoms returned. I'd chase around trying this one and that one. Some worked. Some didn't. Some did one time and not another. I said, "What **is** this?" I went into a funk. My wonderful herbs. Not working? Unbelievable. Finally, I figured it out. Women's hormones seem to ride a delicate cycle. So many things change that cycle. It even changes all by itself. I realized that one day I seemed to need male hormones, maybe the next it was female and a week or month later, maybe I needed both. But, how to know? The answer? Muscle Testing. (See page 32 for details.)

Cool Colleen

Remember *Laura's Special?* That suppository melts up inside you. One lady, Colleen, would use it and it simply wouldn't melt! (Is that why some of us are referred to as cold?) After Colleen balanced her hormones, the suppository melted perfectly.

Many women have problems after they get off the birth control pill. They just can't settle. Some don't have periods. Others have raging tempers and tears. After testing themselves on different herbs and combinations and trying the winners, they've evened out. One lady even wrote me a nice little note. "I took one of the female combinations *(Combination B-5)* and the very next day my allergies cleared up! I haven't sneezed since. I was amazed!"

So was I.

The Itch In The Cellar

Who among us hasn't been struck by vaginal itch? I vividly remember grocery shopping and having to suddenly dive behind a stack of canned tomatoes and scratch. After years of suffering, I found an herbal answer. Here's the recipe:

Garlic Douche

Five buds of *Garlic*. (This is **not** five bulbs. It is five buds pulled off one bulb.) Whip in a blender with one quart of warm water. **Strain** through a paper towel.

I make this up fresh and douche three times a day for three days. (One time may do it.) If it burns too much, I just dilute the mixture a bit. Since a 'dear friend of yours' may reinfect you, have your 'friend' take *Garlic* capsules internally. *Yogurt* would be good, too.

The *Garlic* douche works for nine out of ten women. If it doesn't for you, some women use plain *Yogurt* suppositories, *Liquid Chlorophyl* douches or *Laura's Special.*

Chesta-Mania

And yes, Virginia, there is a breast developer. In my book, *The Outrageous Herb Lady,* I mentioned something that worked for me, but didn't name it. Since then, I've received dozens of letters. "What was that you used?" On lecture tours through the United States and Canada, at every stop it's the same. A lady will sidle up to me and whisper the question in my ear, or sneak a note to me on stage, asking not to be identified, but, "Please. What did you use to grow big breasts?" Here's a list:

Bigger 'n Bigger

Saw Palmetto: Historically grows glandular tissue. In some women it may add a little weight.

Don Quoi

Royal Jelly with *Dong Quoi Extract:* This is the one I used.

All are taken internally.

Nothing works for everyone, however. I found that *Saw Palmetto* seemed to work three out of four times. I've had women call me, so amazed you can hear them smacking slobber. "I'm bigger! Honest! I am! It really works! You can see it! I'm coming right over to show you."

Others said, "Nope, nothing."

However, I've had other women tell me, "It took three years, but it finally worked."

That's the patience of a woman in search of beauty and sex appeal.

Miscarriages

While traveling the midwest on a lecture tour, I met a lady with a sweet baby slung over her shoulder. She told me she had miscarried five babies in a row. With this child she took a certain combination of herbs right from the start and produced a perfect child.

The Baby Keeper

Combination B-6
Golden Seal Root
Capsicum Fruit
False Unicorn Root
Ginger Root
Uva Ursi Leaves
Cramp Bark
Squaw Vine Herb
Blessed Thistle Herb
Red Raspberry Leaves

Another woman, a pretty lady named Ginny, had miscarried several times, three or four months into her pregnancies. The simple addition of *Calcium* and some female herbs, judiciously chosen, brought her a normal pregnancy.

Ginny's Baby Keeper Formula

Single Herbs: *Calcium*

Combination B-1
Comfrey Root
Alfalfa Herb
Oat straw
Irish Moss Plant
Horsetail Herb
Lobelia Herb

Calcium and *Silicon* herbs with trace elements.

Combination B-5
Golden Seal Root
Red Raspberry Leaves
Black Cohosh Root
Queen of the Meadow Herb
Marshmallow Root
Blessed Thistle Herb
Lobelia Herb
Capsicum Fruit
Ginger Root

Traditionally used to balance hormones. Be cautious with hormone type herbs during pregnancy. I'd muscle test.

Miscarriage Thwarted

Linda started spotting nine or ten weeks into her pregnancy. She immediately went to bed and stayed there, drinking *False Unicorn Tea* spiked with *Lobelia*. Within days the bleeding stopped.

It's such a traumatic experience, both emotionally and physically, for a woman to miscarry. It's a common occurance, but that doesn't make it easy.

Not all miscarriages can be stopped with herbs, nor should they be. Herbalists often say that herbs will hold the fetus if it should be held and help it out if it is imperfect.

To Conceive Or Not To Conceive

Lisa had multiple problems. Acne, constipation, tiredness, pale blood. She was about 28, had never been married but had had several long-term relationships. She had no children. "I've never used birth control and I've never gotten pregnant." After a month or so on a good herbal program, Lisa **was** pregnant. And mad as wild fleas. She had expected glorious health but not a baby too!

I've seen this happen several times while women are on an herbal program. It makes sense. Clean up the body and let it repair itself and you've got Mother Nature hopping for joy. If a woman is a poor physical vehicle for a child, it's nature's general rule to prevent conception.

I tried for two and one half years to conceive my daughter, Summer. Nothing happened. My husband at the time, confessed to my father that he had become utterly worn out. I know the desperation a woman feels. The longing for a baby. All the tears and sadness. The endless doctor visits and hair-raising suggestions given, from trying **it** on certain days, to hormone shots and major operations.

My ex-husband and I even slept for several years in a bed with the foot end up on cinder blocks. The idea was that the sperm would run up hill and stay there. All I got was uncomfortable.

Finally the specialist I was seeing said, "OK, you've got *"Multiple Belly Jig Syndrome"* and we're going to have to go in and cut **this** out and rearrange **that** and do some slicing here, some rewiring and oh shoot...you'll be out of the hospital in two or three weeks."

I said, "Heck you will and heck I will," and tried another route.

I consulted an herbalist. He said, "Take these herbs and give it six months or so."

Within **one** month I was looking at the breakfast my mother-in-law handed me. One runny egg! And running frantically from the house.

...I was pregnant.

Here's what I would do now, if I couldn't conceive:

I'd clean my body using the *Comfrey-Pepsin Cleanse.*

I'd repair my body, using *Builders* of my choice.

At the same time, or a bit later, I would work to balance my hormones.

If I had a problem like endometriosis, cysts or ratty fallopian tubes, I'd be sure to add *Laura's Special.*

The Man

If you think it could be your macho husband:

The Macho Male Program

Single Herbs:

Lecithin	Found abundantly in semen.
Zinc	Used by men for sex and the prostate.

Combination B-23
Siberian Ginseng Root
Echinacea Root
Saw Palmetto Berries
Gotu Kola Herb
Damiana Leaves
Sarsaparilla Root
Periwinkle Herb
Garlic Bulb
Capsicum Fruit
Chickweed Herb

Traditionally rebuilds the sexual organs. Also keeps the man's interest up.

The Magic Charm

And for those of you who have given up hope, here's something to gladden your hearts and make you doubt the truth of my stories for sure.

Three years ago a witch came to see me. A bona fide, regular, run-of-the-mill witch. She was 72, had long, dark, dyed black hair and was stout. She wore black, of course, and around her neck swung a bevy of clanking, swishing pentagrams (five pointed star used as a magical symbol) and regular stars. She smelled sour, as witches might be imagined to smell. I read her eyes and she read my palm.

"You'll have three marriages," she pronounced, "and an exciting life."

I was impressed.

She flitted off, herbal blood purifiers in hand. I didn't see her again for three years, but her young friend, Arica, kept me informed.

"She's still taking her herbs," Arica said, "And doing great. Now she wants to try some others. She wants some herbs to balance her hormones. She doesn't want brittle bones."

Still later, Arica gave me another report, "Boy! She says those herbs have really fixed her up, Venus. She's looking for a boyfriend."

Later I heard she found one. In fact, several.

Two weeks ago, Arica came to me. "Venus, sit down. I've got gossip." I sat. "You know my friend, the witch? She's 75 years old, right? And she's got a live-in lover who's 35, right?"

Well, that last part was news to me, but I like younger men myself. I sure couldn't fault her for her taste.

"Venus," Arica put her hand on my shoulders as if to steady me. "She's **pregnant!**"

"What?" I hollered. "What? What? What?"

"Yes, yes, yes," Arica chanted. "It's not a tumor. She's been to the doctor. They want to abort but she says no. She wants this baby. She's never had a child.

"Peel me off the floor," I begged. "Don't tell me we did this to her."

Arica grinned. "Yep. She swears it was the *Damiana.*

I'm Pregnant

There's a picture of me after I had my daughter, Summer. My family keeps it just to devil me. I'm lying in bed, my hair sprung out in dry jabs. My eyes hang low like a blood hound's and my flabby, white arms are slung loosely on the covers. I look like they dragged me around the back yard a few times. That's how I felt, too. Droves of friends came to see me. I'd say, "Mother, keep those people away from me."

My poor mother entertained them for hours. I was simply too exhausted to make small talk.

If I had it to do over again, I'd prevent the dry falling hair. The cavities. The exhaustion. I'd also want to protect my developing baby from mental and physical problems. I'd take herbs the **entire** nine months instead of stopping them after I conceived.

Making A Baby

Combination B-1 Comfrey Root Alfalfa Herb Oat Straw Irish Moss Plant Horsetail Herb Lobelia Herb	A rich source of *Calcium* for strong bones and teeth. If you don't have enough *Calcium* and trace elements for the child, there goes your own hair and teeth.
Single Herbs: Kelp	Provides minerals, trace elements and traditioally helps prevent birth defects and mental retardation.
Combination B-3 Kelp Plant Dandelion Root Alfalfa Herb	Many mothers feel these elements also prevent birth defects and mental retardation.

Continued...

Red Raspberry Leaves	Considered **the** women's herb. I would take it all through my pregnancy.
Vitamin E	

A good *Vitamin* and *Mineral Capsule* or *Tablet.*

A specially formulated *Mineral* and *Trace Element Combination.*

The Baby's Coming

Nellie called me, bubbling over. "My daughter went into the hospital to have her first baby. It was 3 p.m. The nurse checked her and said to me, 'Go on home, dearie...this baby isn't coming 'til midnight.' Well I'll tell you—the baby shot out at 4:30 p.m.!" She paused for breath. "The doctor said, 'I can't believe it. This woman gave birth like a woman having her tenth child!' At the same time, my daughter's two girl friends had all kinds of trouble having their babies."

Nellie's daughter had taken the following combination during the last five to six weeks of her pregnancy:

Combination B-21 *Black Cohosh Root* *Squaw Vine Herb* *Lobelia Herb* *Pennyroyal Herb* *Red Raspberry Leaves*	Historically shortens labor and makes the birth easier.

Labor

Here's some odd facts and tidbits used by women through the centuries:

Blue Cohosh: Was used by Indian women to dilate the cervix and hasten birth.

Lobelia: As a douche used for pain **before** the water broke. Women also rubbed *Lobelia Extract* on the abdomen for pain and put a small amount under their tongues.

Red Raspberry Tea: Was drunk while in labor to make it easier and prevent excessive bleeding.

Vitamin E: Women, now, often take this every hour while having contractions. It supplies oxygen for the baby if there's fetal distress.

Babies And Children

You can pretty much treat babies like real human beings. Just use smaller amounts of herbs. Remember, if you're nursing, whatever you take, goes into your child. Be cautious of cleansing yourself too heavily unless you like changing diapers. I know how nervous a new mother can be with a baby. I once sat up all night with Summer and Dr. Spock. I was sure her bowel movement was the wrong color. While she gurgled and played, I rocked and stared out the blackened windows, waiting for her to pass on.

Crying—Restless

Sometimes you get a baby who cries a lot. One couple I know rubs *Lobelia Extract* down the baby's spine before bed and often gives a few drops internally. They also rub it on her gums when she's teething.

Our Helen, of *Hairball* fame, had a couple who came to visit for three days and stayed for three months. Their crying child kept her up all night. In desperation, she fixed him a strong slug of *Catnip Tea* and he slept solid. She later alternated with *Chamomile*.

Diaper Rash

Diane kept her baby on *Yellow Dock Tea* to clear and keep diaper rash away. Lori uses *Aloe Vera Jel* directly on the skin.

Teething

Last night I spent some time with Stephanie. We sat by the Christmas tree as she fed her little baby, Suzanne. Suzanne kicked and squirmed and cried. Obviously she was uncomfortable and unhappy. "She's trying to cut teeth," her mom explained. "They haven't popped through yet, and she's so miserable." I suggested an herbal combination that's high in *Calcium*. Often, a baby has trouble cutting teeth because of a *Calcium* lack. If you get a concentrated form of the combination, it will go through a nipple. Otherwise, make a strong tea. Or, take it yourself and nurse the baby.

Suzanne's Teeth Relief

Combination B-1	*Irish Moss Plant*	
Comfrey Root	Horsetail Herb	
Alfalfa Herb	Lobelia Herb	Natural *Calcium*
Oat Straw		

Digestion

If you're giving your baby cow's milk, you might try adding *Papaya Powder* or *Papaya* with *Mint*. These herbs supposedly make the milk more like mother's.

Cradle Cap

One mother had a 9 year old son with crusty cradle cap. They'd been everywhere, even to Mexico looking for a cure. Finally, his mother rubbed a high quality *Jojoba Oil* on his scalp and left it on over night. The next day she washed his hair with a good **herbal shampoo**. She repeated this process daily and after three days the cradle cap was gone.

Rotten Children

There was Martha. Two and one half years old with a finger always up her nose. She never walked into a room. She was always **dragged** into a room. And she whined. And cried. Hid in her mother's skirts and kicked. She was generally sick with something. The entire time I knew her she snuffled. Her mother finally decided that with all her allergies, colds and flus, her immune system must be shot. She gave her:

Rotten Martha's Special

Fenugreek and *Thyme:* Historically, *Fenugreek* is used to clear mucus and infections and *Thyme* repairs the thymus gland, which is considered the seat of the immune system.

Vitamin A: The infection fighter.

Vitamin C

Zinc: Used for preventing infections.

Pau d'Arco: Builds the immune system.

It worked. Martha is now clever and cute and only picks her nose part-time.

Terrible Adolescents

I'm going to tell you something that may save your emotional life. One evening when Summer was about 11, I climbed the stairs to her room. I found her slumped on her bed. "What's the matter, Tum-Tum?" I asked. She began to cry. Then scream. She flew into an uninhibited frenzy, rolling and kicking on the bed. Then, she got on her knees and hopped up and down. I was alarmed. This wasn't my calm, happy daughter who woke up singing every morning. Finally, she stopped flailing. Looking at me and breathing hard, she said, "I hate you mother. I have for two months now." She broke into guilty sobbing. "I don't know why. I don't want to, Mom. I don't know what's wrong with me!"

Another mother, Karen, came to visit shortly after. "Venus, you've got to help me. My two boys, 11 and 12, are in love with girls! They're driving me crazy. I speak to them and they stare off into space with their mouths hanging open. They're acting like they're not all there. They've become utterly worthless."

Fortunately, Dr. Christopher supplies an answer. Karen and I tried it and it works. Her boys are now playing baseball and Summer is again singing every morning. As long as I keep her on the herbs she's cheerful and productive.

I've had a number of parents ask me, "So how long should my kids take these?" I tell them frankly, "Until they leave home."

Emotional Reprieve

Red Raspberry Capsules
Blessed Thistle Capsules

Dr. Christopher suggests three each daily for both boys and girls.

PART V

Herbs For The Serious Physical Problems

"Some people think that doctors and nurses can put scrambled eggs back into the shell."

Dorothy Canfield

Those Serious Problems

Most ailments are easy to fix. Doctors know that 80 to 90 percent of the time the body heals itself, if you just wait it out.

Following are some herb programs to help the body help itself. Once again, these are not to be taken as diagnoses or prescriptions. When in doubt see your doctor.

Lungs, Sinus And Allergies

Breathing seems to be one of the necessities of life. Yet, many people have trouble breathing. They smoke, have allergies, asthma, emphysema, croup, pneumonia or bronchitis. Just yesterday I talked with a 20 year old who's attending college in Louisiana. He explained he'd gotten a cough since he'd moved there. He coughed frequently for me to prove his point.

"It's pretty moist down there," I remarked. I recalled how when I'd vacationed there, I'd left my toothbrush on the washbasin one evening. It had grown mold over night. That impressed me.

The fellow carried a few herbs back to Louisiana with him. A combination used for deep-lung cleansing and *Pau d'Arco* and *Fenugreek* and *Thyme.* The latter herbs are traditionally used to kill virus, molds and bacteria.

Bronchial Problems

Grace told me she woke in the night during a big storm. She could barely breathe. Her "lungs were rattling and swooshing." She panicked, then grabbed an herb book. It's advice: Take *Cayenne* and *Ginger Root.* She did and breathed easily, again.

Asthma

The first thing most people need to do is build up their nervous systems.[22] They often add an **extract** of:

Combination B-18		
Valerian Root	*Black Walnut Hulls*	
Aniseed	*Licorice*	For instant relaxation
Lobelia Herb	*Ginger Root*	
Brigham Tea		Continued...

22. Advice from Dr. Christopher

Then slowly they begin using a deep-lung cleansing combination such as:

> **Combination C-16**
> *Comfrey Root*
> *Marshmallow Root*   Deep-lung cleanser
> *Mullein Leaves*
> *Slippery Elm Bark*
> *Lobelia Herb*

They start slowly because, sometimes, the moving toxins can contribute to an asthmatic attack. For security they keep *Peppermint Tea* and *Lobelia Extract* in their cupboards. When an attack begins they sip strong *Peppermint Tea* and every ten minutes squirt *Lobelia Extract* under their tongues. A number of people have told me. "It opened me right up and I could breathe. Saved a trip to the hospital."

Emphysema

Ilene's father takes capsules of *Pau d'Arco* throughout the day. He says it helps him breathe easier, just like his medicine did.

Other people also take *Aloe Vera Juice* hoping to cut down on scar tissue.

Mullein is historically used for lung inflammations and here is a combination which tends to bring up mucus:

> **Combination C-18**
> *Comfrey Root*   Brings out mucus
> *Fenugreek Seeds*

An herbal combination to deep clean the lungs is often used, along with a good combination for tissue repair like:

> **Combination B-1**
> *Comfrey Root*
> *Alfalfa Herb*
> *Oat Straw*   Tissue repair
> *Irish Moss Plant*
> *Horsetail Herb*
> *Lobelia Herb*

A *Traditional Deep-lung Cleanser* in addition to **Combination C-16** and **Combination C-18** is:

```
┌─────────────────────────────────────────────────────────┐
│   Combination C-17                                      │
│   Comfrey Root                                          │
│   Marshmallow Root        Deep-lung cleanser            │
│   Lobelia Herb                                          │
│   Chickweed Herb                                        │
│   Mullein Leaves                                        │
└─────────────────────────────────────────────────────────┘
```

Sinus

Here's our Helen again, of *Hairball* fame. She said her nose was plugged up one night and nothing would unplug it. She took matters in hand and grabbed an extract she normally used for hearing and ear problems.[23] "I shot it up my nose," she said grandly, "and down my throat. It worked."

I like having Helen around. She's willing to experiment. She's also had dozens of health problems so we have something to experiment **on**. She gets a case of sinus now and then. Her solution? "I get *Liquid Chlorophyll* and put some *Cayenne Pepper* in it. Then I snuff it up my nose. Oh," she trills, "it works great."

People with sinus generally take one of the *Deep Lung Cleansers* mentioned above. Sometimes they find a combination used for allergies helps tremendously:

```
┌─────────────────────────────────────────────────────────┐
│                  Sinus Or Allergies                     │
│                                                         │
│   Combination BC-10          OR                         │
│   Golden Seal Root                                      │
│   Capsicum Fruit             Combination BC-11          │
│   Parsley Root               Blessed Thistle Herb       │
│   Desert (Brigham) Tea Herb  Black Cohosh Root          │
│   Marshmallow Root           Skullcap Herb              │
│   Chaparral Herb             Pleurisy Root              │
│   Lobelia Herb                                          │
│   Burdock Root                                          │
└─────────────────────────────────────────────────────────┘
```

However, when they really get serious, they've got to **snort**.

Sometimes the sinuses are so bad a person feels throbbing in the teeth, the face, the forehead. Mucus is packed in the sinus cavity and common sense says it needs to come out.

A lady came to see me a few mornings ago, collecting the herbs *Goldenseal Root* and *Bayberry Bark Root*.

I remarked, "Didn't you just get those same herbs several days ago?"

She answered, "Yes. Remember I got them for a man friend whose

---

23. See Appendix I

93

nose and sinus were so plugged up he felt crazy? Well, you said if you had his problem you'd take a combination of *Herbs For Infections*[24] and another for sinus and snort the sinus herbs right up your nose ... Remember?"

"Yeah," I said. "I remember saying I'd take the other herbs internally and sniff the last two (*Goldenseal* and *Bayberry*) up my nose ..." My voice trailed off and I looked at her questioningly.

"Well," said the lady enthused. "He loves it. He loves it!"

I was surprised. "Yeah? He **loves** snorting that stuff? Nobody else does. They use it as a last resort. Is he any better?"

"Oh, of course," she answered. "He got better right away. He just loves to snort this stuff."

I can almost guarantee, **you won't.**

Allergies

Allergies generally respond to the same herbs as any lung problem we've mentioned. A normal program might be:

Lung
Cleanser

Single Herbs:
Bee Pollen
Comfrey

AND

Combination C-16
Comfrey Root
Marshmallow Root
Mullein Leaves
Slippery Elm Bark
Lobelia Herb

Historically used
for allergies

OR

Combination C-17
Comfrey Root
Marshmallow Root
Lobelia Herb
Chickweed Herb
Mullein Leaves

OR

Combination BC-10
Golden Seal Root
Capsicum Fruit
Parsley Root
Desert (Brigham) Tea Herb
Marshmallow Root
Chaparral Herb
Lobelia Herb
Burdock Root

Lung
Cleanser

Relief will generally be felt in a matter of days or weeks. After a year of body cleansing many people find their allergies have gone forever. Claire very simply got rid of her cat allergy by taking *Alfalfa*.

The Allergic Grass Hunter

Jack has an interesting allergy. He says, "I'm allergic to marijuana. I have to take a special combination of herbs that people take who have food allergies:

24. See Appendix I

94

I have to take it when I drive uptown. Many people cut pipe tobacco with grass and it sends me into fits. Once I was coming over from Catalina Island on the boat. I got this horrible reaction. When I react I look like I'm smoking myself. My eyes blur and ache, my head hurts and things get foggy. I knew someone must be transporting marijuana because I felt so incredibly bad. My dad told the ship's captain who called the coast guard. The coast guard found and arrested the two guys. They had wads of "grass" in several satchels.

Insect Allergies

"My husband, Dale, is awfully allergic to bees," Fran said. "When he's stung, he has to go to the hospital, get shots and go on a heart monitor. It's scary. He got stung the other day and I immediately gave him eight capsules of a *Blood Purifier,* 8000 units of *Vitamin C* and lots of *Black Cohosh.* He recovered with no swelling and no hospital."

Arthritis and Gout

Vicki is a checker at the supermarket. She's about 50 and has been checking groceries for a long time. Checkers spend their years standing up. Which was fine with Vicki until she developed arthritis in her knee. She had to go on disability and prepared herself for a knee operation. Then, she discovered herbs. Her knee is fine now. No operation and she's back at work.

Another woman had arthritis for decades. She was bent at the elbows and knees. When she walked, she looked like a monkey. She had finally advanced to a wheelchair and dependence on others for her needs. After four months on an herbal program she was out Christmas shopping. She gave the wheelchair away and took up living.

People often report startling results with herbs and arthritis. Many get a lot of relief. And a few get nothing.

Are you aware that at the turn of the century, different doctors and researchers at different times discovered a bacillus (a living creature) involved with rheumatoid arthritis? They wrote books and pamphlets and research papers on their findings.

Do you think anyone listened to them? Of course not. This is the World's Motto: "Let's stick with the tried and true even if it doesn't work."

Here's a program many sufferers use:

Repairs Tissue

Combination B-1
Comfrey Root
Alfalfa Herb
Oat Straw
Irish Moss Plant
Horsetail Herb
Lobelia Herb

AND

Combination BC-2
Bromelain
Yucca Root
Comfrey Root
Alfalfa Herb
Black Cohosh Root
Yarrow Flowers
Capsicum Fruit
Chaparral Herb
Lobelia Herb
Burdock Root
Centaury Herb

Continued...

OR

Combination BC-1
Hydrangea Root
Desert (Brigham) Tea Herb
Chaparral Herb
Yucca Root
Black Cohosh Root
Capsicum Fruit
Black Walnut Hulls
Valerian Root
Sarsaparilla Root
Lobelia Herb
Skullcap Herb
Burdock Root
Wild Lettuce Leaves
Wormwood Herb

AND

Single Herbs:
Licorice Root: Acts like cortisone
Black Walnut: Historically kills unwelcome creatures
Pau d'Arco

One old man found relief from arthritic pain this way:

"I take four *Yucca* capsules with one cup of fresh or frozen grapefruit juice, one half hour before breakfast and again at bedtime...on an empty stomach. After I've taken this for two to three weeks, my pain goes away. I know acid juices are supposed to bother me but this doesn't. Maybe it works because the combination dissolves the buildup in my joints?"

Another woman reports, "My friend Jane is 22 years old. She's had arthritis for years. When she began nursing her baby she took *Blessed Thistle* and *Marshmallow.* She wanted to have lots of rich milk. She got that, but her arthritis went away and it's never come back."

That Gouty Guy

Occasionally my dear father gets gout. He gets it in his big toes. He sits around with his toes up in the air and moans. He's a sorry sight, but what can I do? I can't force herbs on the man. Mother won't hold him down for me.

Diane has better luck with her dad. She gives him *Safflower* and *Dandelion* and the gout disappears.

What are we going to do with **my** father?

Kidneys And Bladder

Jack And The Bladder

Jack had constant pain in his kidneys and bladder and blood in his urine. Several trips to the doctor failed to halt the pain or find anything wrong. Desperate, Jack finally took eight *Marshmallow Root* capsules a day, strong and slippery *Slippery Elm* tea and an herbal combination for kidneys and bladder.[25] One week later, he was fine.

The Regular, Yearly Bladder Infection

Many women suffer periodically with bladder infections. Jack's program works just as well for them.

Enraged Kidney

After a seemingly endless flight home from Europe, I developed an enraged kidney. It felt like it was bouncing around inside my lower back, screaming and kicking. I could barely sit, stand or lie down! One day on *Jack's Program*...heavy...with added *Parsley,* and I lived!

Bed Wetters

As a kid, I always wet the bed when I ate watermelon. It was hard to give up bed wetting as I got older because it was a family tradition. "Venus always wets the bed when she eats watermelon."

Once, we all went to visit Grandma. We had watermelon. Later, there weren't enough beds, so my two sisters and I slept together. I got the middle. About midnight, I woke up. I had to go. Boy, did I have to go. But, it was so warm in that bed. And I was tucked in the middle and it'd be such a bother to clamber over my sisters. And after all, everybody **knew** that Venus **always** wet the bed when she ate watermelon. So. I wet the bed. I can remember how warm it was as it soaked my nightgown and spread out and soaked my sisters. And how mad they were!! It was a real mess but I got away with it because it was a tradition.

If you'd like to get rid of these kinds of family rituals you might try:

25. See Appendix I

Jack's Program

Bladder and Kidneys

Combination BC-22
Juniper Berries
Parsley Herb
Uva Ursi Leaves
Dandelion Root
Chamomile Flowers

OR

Combination BC-23
Golden Seal Root
Juniper Berries
Uva Ursi Leaves
Parsley Herb
Ginger Root
Marshmallow Root
Lobelia Herb

Bladder and Kidneys

AND

Combination B-17
Black Cohosh Root
Capsicum Fruit
Valerian Root
Mistletoe Herb
Lady's Slipper Root
Lobelia Herb
Skullcap Herb
Hops Flowers
Wood Betony Herb

OR

Combination B-16
Black Cohosh Root
Capsicum Fruit
Valerian Root
Mistletoe Herb
Ginger Root
St. Johnswort Herb
Hops Flowers
Wood Betony Herb

OR

Single Herbs:
Parsley

Nerve Repair

Nerve Repair

Both **Combination B-17** and **Combination B-16** are used with bed wetters. Sometimes the child's nerves aren't quite mature to these areas of the body.

Liver And Gallbladder

Gallstones

Reliable sources will say, "You just don't **pass** gallstones! Impossible." Let me tell you, on a gallbladder flush you pass **something**."

I had been on a cleanse for three days. I didn't realize it was a gallbladder flush. I can't remember exactly what I thought it was supposed to be and do, but I certainly was surprised. I'd just had a bowel movement. I turned to look before I flushed and my gawd. I'd passed some jewels. Emeralds or aquamarines! My hand flew to my heart. Jewels! I'd passed jewels! Then reason took over. I looked closer. "Shoot. They must be gallstones." I felt pretty foolish but mainly disappointed.

We're Rich

Ludmilla and Isaac are back with another incredible story. Ludmilla, the herbalist, tells us:

"I've taken other liver and gallbladder flushes, but none as exciting as Isaac's. We did it together. For three days we drank gallons of apple juice. On the third night we each downed a cup of fresh lemon juice, a cup of olive oil and a cathartic. What fun. Then we raced off to bed and lay on our right sides for an hour or so with our knees to our chests. I felt a little nauseous and panicky. I grabbed an herb book and hugged it close. Surely I wouldn't die from this. The herbalists in the book spoke of it as a regular ho-hum procedure.

Morning broke. So did Isaac. He was up and out of bed as though shot from a gun. He roared to the bathroom and slammed the door. "Ah, oh," I thought. "It must be big. I don't want to miss this." I threw back the covers and raced to the door.

"Let me in, Isaac," I begged.

"No," he said. The sound of a 1000 marbles spraying against porcelain ripped the stillness. I pounded the door.

"Isaac! Isaac! What's happening? What's happening?" Silence. Then a muffled explosion and the sound of rabbit pellets flying. I opened the door and flew in. Isaac looked disgusted. "Oh, boy!" I shouted. "Something must have come out, Isaac. Let's look!"

After a stony stare, his curiousity prodded him off the pot. He mumbled, "Of all the women I could have married..."

We peered intently into the toilet. What a haul! What a treasure trove! Assuring each other that what we were doing was certainly disgusting, we scooped up and ladled and counted. At final count, Isaac had passed at least 50 dark, waxy, green balls. With no pain. He was quite pleased with himself.

"Bottle them up," he said. "I want to show them off."

They were bottled and kept in our refrigerator for several months.They were a favorite item at my herb classes. They met an untimely end, however. One evening I found the bottle uncapped and the stones overturned into our tuna casserole masquerading as peas.

(Caution: If you know you have gallstones, check with your doctor before trying this flush.)

Don's Liver-Gallbladder Flush

This is from Don, an herbalist in Arizona.

Liver-Gallbladder Flush

Combination BC-3	OR
Red Beet Root	
Dandelion Root	**Combination BC-4**
Parsley Herb	Barberry Root Bark
Horsetail (Shavegrass) Herb	Ginger Root
Liverwort Herb	Cramp Bark
Birch Leaves	Fennel Seeds
Lobelia Herb	Peppermint Leaves
Blessed Thistle Herb	Wild Yam Root
Angelica Root	Catnip Herb
Chamomile Flowers	
Gentian Root	
Golden Rod Herb	

"I take one of these combinations for four to six weeks to prepare for my cleanse, but that's optional.

"**First Day:** Upon arising I take 16 ounces of pure, unsweetened apple juice. Every two hours I take eight ounces of apple juice. I don't eat any food. If I begin to feel weak, headachy or too hungry, I take an herbal combination every two hours that consists of: *Licorice Root, Hawthorn Berries* and *Fennel Seeds* (*Combinations B-35*). I use *Cascara Sagrada* to stimulate bile flow and keep the colon moving. If I don't have several bowel movements a day, I take enemas or colonics. It is **most** important that my bowel be kept open and moving.

"**Second Day:** Repeat the first day. Then, one-half hour before bedtime, I take two to four ounces of *Olive Oil* mixed with two or more tablespoons of fresh *Lemon* or *Grapefruit Juice.* It's poured one glass to another at least 20 times to mix well before I drink it. If I feel nauseated, I take an enema. Within 24 hours I usually expel stones with my bowel movement. I sometimes repeat this program in two weeks for further results. Sometimes a person won't pass anything the first time or even the second. But by the third, holy-moly!"

Personally, for a while before and for several months after this flush, I take one of the liver-gallbladder herbal combinations Don mentions, plus several of the straight herbs: *Dandelion, Aloe Vera, Yellow Dock, Chlorophyll.*

The above herbs are used equally well by people with **liver** problems.

A woman named Fern visited me several years ago. Her 28-year-old husband was dying of an un-named liver disease. The doctors had called Fern in and told her there was nothing more she, or the hospital could do for him. Eight months on the above herbs, including the combinations and he was well. I heard from her a few days ago. "We recently went to France and he drank more wine than I did."

Blood Sugar

Problems here can lead to depression and energy lacks.

The Sinking Disease

It was hot when Katie blew into my office. Her hair was stuck to her head and she pawed the desk frantically. "I've got to have some liquid *Chlorophyll.* Right now. It helps me survive the heat. I guess I need it for my blood sugar. It helps me retain my *Calcium* and absorb the herbs. When I stop taking it, I notice a big difference in four or five days."

Abby told me she'd been so crazy with low blood sugar that she'd been "in and out of mental hospitals. The very day I went on an herb program my head cleared up and I've been sane ever since."

My brother, Art, consented to let me herbally experiment with him. He'd been diagnosed as hypoglycemic. After several weeks he said, "This is the first time in my life that I feel in touch with reality. I feel like my feet touch the ground and I'm not confused."

Art Used:

Combination B-11
Licorice Root
Safflower Flowers
Dandelion Root
Horseradish Root

AND, OR

Combination B-12
Soy Protein
Capsicum Fruit
Red Clover Tops

Some people carry *Licorice Root Extract* with them. (*Licorice* is historically used for the adrenals and stress.) When they feel themselves sinking, they whip out the bottle and take a squirt.)

Personally, I prefer what I call *"Crazy Tea."* I drink it when I feel confused, dumb and crazy.

Crazy Tea

Combination B-13
Peppermint Leaves
Licorice Root
Cinnamon Bark
Spearmint Leaves

Diabetes

There was a huge lady who said she had diabetes. She hadn't been able to feel her legs under her, for years. She had trouble walking because she couldn't tell if she was hitting the ground. She began taking *Aloe Vera Juice* and working out on a mini-trampoline. She can now feel her legs.

My sister-in-law, Mary Ellen, takes *Pau d'Arco, Goldenseal* and a combination of herbs for the pancreas. She says her blood sugar is consistently dropping and she's losing weight.

Many diabetics report excellent results with these herbs. Many say they are able to gradually cut back on their insulin and some eventually stop completely.

Single Herbs:
Aloe Vera Juice
Pau d'Arco
Goldenseal

Combination BC-16
Golden Seal Root
Juniper Berries
Uva Ursi Leaves
Huckleberry Leaves
Mullein Leaves
Comfrey Root
Yarrow Flowers
Garlic Bulb
Capsicum Fruit
Dandelion Root
Marshmallow Root
Buchu Leaves
Bistort Root
Licorice Root

Used for
the Pancreas

Heart, Blood Pressure and Circulation

Heart Disease Is Very Popular

But, realistically, it's one of the easiest problems to prevent or fix.

I'd had trouble with my heart since I was a teenager. I'd sometimes feel like there was a moth flapping frantically in my chest. Several years ago the symptoms got worse. Sometimes the moth would turn into an elephant and he'd **sit** on my chest. Occasionally,it was hard to breathe. Other times I found myself breathing heavily even while sitting and minding my own business. This progressed to sudden attacks of violently racing heart which left me terrified and bewildered. Soon I found it difficult to walk up stairs without becoming winded. Working in my garden became an impossibility. I'd steadfastly ignored these heart symptoms for years in favor of worry over cancer. But, at last I had to face facts. I was quite liable to drop dead before cancer got me.

After one wildly flapping and long-lasting attack, I wrote out a will. I penned it on scratch paper and tucked it in my underwear drawer. Then, I sat down to worry. Dropping dead was something I felt I could handle but being a cripple was not. Already involved with herbs, I began to study those traditionally used for the heart. I decided on *Hawthorn Berries*. One and a half months after I began taking them, I was free of **all** symptoms except occasional heart palpitations. A year or so later a friend of mine, Judie, a woman of about 35, called to say she'd just gotten out of the hospital. She had been there with a racing heart and palpitations. I told her my story but warned her to give the herbs a month or two to make a difference. She called me one week later. "It took only three days!" (I keep telling you guys...we're all different.)

Heart Throbs

Then there was Nadine. She's a lady about 50. She was in a car accident that crushed her chest and heart. At the time I met her the doctors had done everything they could for her. As she said, "My heart always pounds at 200 beats a minute. The doctors tell me I could drop dead any time." Nadine went on a full herbal heart program including *Lobelia Extract*. She later said, *"Lobelia* helps stop the racing and palpitating when I've slacked off on my herbs." She now says, "I'm totally well. As long as I keep taking a minimum amount of the herbs, I'm fine." She's gone on to own and manage a string of art galleries along with her own artistic career. She also has a new...and handsome...man everytime I see her.

Dave, a man in his 60s, told me his doctor had discussed seriously, the prospect of his having open-heart surgery. Six months later, after extensive testing, the doctors can find nothing wrong with Dave's heart. Dave, of course, had put himself on an herbal program.

For Typical Heart Hunger

| Supplies Potassium | Single Herbs:
Hawthorn Berries
Trace Minerals
Chlorophyll

Combination B-32
Kelp
Dulse
Watercress
Wild Cabbage
Horseradish
Horsetail | Combination B-1
Comfrey Root
Alfalfa Herb
Oat Straw
Irish Moss Plant
Horsetail Herb
Lobelia Herb

Combination B-36
Concentrated
  Hawthorn
Vitamin E
Selenium
Apple Pectin | Repairs Tissues

Historically repairs the Heart and Arteries |

Of course, stress adds to heart problems and can cause them. Using iridology, I once looked into a lady's left eye and saw a whitish patch over the heart area in her iris. "Do you ever get pains in your chest?" I asked. "No," she said. I had just met the woman so didn't want to pry, but I had to say, "Well...often when I see that it means pain or stress." By the end of our talk the woman had admitted to me, "My heart is broken. My boyfriend just left me." Can you see how people die of broken hearts? If I had a broken heart, or stress, I would hit the *Calcium* bottle hard and also the herbs for stress.

When I was being plagued with my heart problems, I had a dream. I was in a large auditorium. An American Indian man sat in one of the seats. I approached him and asked what I could do about my heart. He got up, turned away from me and said, "You won't listen." He walked off. I ran after him, begging. He faced me. "Sage," he said. When I woke up I rifled through all my herb books, reading about *Sage*. None suggested it for the heart. I decided, "Silly dream," and didn't use the herb. Several years later, a medical researcher who had just returned from China said, "Over there they use *Sage* for palpitations and other heart problems."

A friend of mine, Reba, fat and 30, confided to me that she was worried. She was having pains down her left arm, a feeling in her chest like her heart was stopping and spasms.

"I've got three little kids," she said. "Dream me a dream." I did. I found Reba eating piles of *Black Walnuts,* hulls and all, from a tall grocery bag. When reporting my dream, I said, "All I can imagine is that you need lots of something in *Black Walnut Hulls.* Maybe *Potassium?* Reba, unlike me, listened to my dream. She began taking *Black Walnut Hulls* (in powdered form). She added in *Lobelia* to relax her and *Hawthorn Berries,* just in case. Three years later she's had no further problem.

Palpitations...Or "Dear John"

We were at a convention. I was in our hotel room, standing at the window watching ice hang from the trees. Keith, my husband at the time, was attending a lecture several blocks away. The day was peaceful. I was enjoying the silence. Then suddenly the moth in my chest fluttered her wings. Palpitations. Nothing to worry about. *Calcium* usually quieted them. This time, it didn't. The wings flapped again. And again. Then they fluttered in a semi-steady rhythm. I'd never had so many palpitations and so close together. I stood up straight and held perfectly still. It didn't help. I paced a bit hysterically. The fluttering stopped.

I turned on the TV and sat on the bed. If I was very quiet and concentrated on something else it wouldn't come again. It came. Panic. Should I have Keith paged? Have him leave the lecture and come to me? It was an important talk he was attending, one he didn't want to miss. What could he do for me? Pat my hand? No, I'd write a note. "Dear Keith," I penned. "I'm sorry I died. I didn't want to bother you. My heart just gave out. It wasn't painful. Just some hysteria. Tell Summer I love her." I lay down and put the note on my chest and eventually fell asleep.

An hour or so later when Keith came in, I was up and around, cheerily changing my clothes. The fluttering had stopped.

"Guess what," I said, trying to put concern in my voice. "I almost died while you were gone." Keith looked at me. "I did, really," I said and detailed my experience.

"Why didn't you have me paged?" Keith demanded.

"Hey, listen," I countered. "I wrote you a note."

Keith looked at me, stupified. "You thought you were dying..." he said, measuring out the words, "and...you... wrote me...a **note**?"

Since then I've made a study of palpitations. I've found that mine usually come when my hormones are out of sync. *Sarsaparilla,* an herb that contains the hormone progesterone, usually stops them. At other times it's *Siberian Ginseng* (more progesterone.) And sometimes I need *Black Cohosh,* which acts like estrogen. I use muscle testing to see which I need.

107

Occasionally, I think low blood sugar causes my palpitations and I then use several combinations of herbs, a couple of capsules every three to four hours:

Used With Blood Sugar Problems

Combination B-11
Licorice Root
Safflower Flowers
Dandelion Root
Horseradish Root

Combination B-12
Soy Protein
Capsicum Fruit
Red Clover Tops

If the palpitations seem stress related, I use *Lobelia* or *Valerian Root*. I use the extracts if possible, because they work faster.

Some people tell me *Hawthorn Extract* under the tongue works for them. *Hawthorn* feeds the heart.

High Blood Pressure

Nine out of ten people who use the correct herbs seem to get relief from high blood pressure. They often switch combinations back and forth:

Combination BC-18
Hawthorn Berries
Capsicum Fruit
Garlic Bulb

OR

Combination BC-20
Garlic Bulb
Capsicum Fruit
Parsley Root
Ginger Root
Siberian Ginseng Root
Golden Seal Root

OR

Combination BC-19
Garlic Bulb
Capsicum Fruit

Those who have high blood pressure from kidney problems often do well with *Blue Cohosh*. I'd also work on my kidney herbs if it were me.

Occasionally, people report success with *Siberian Ginseng*. If all else fails, I'd clean out my blood stream with blood purifiers:

	Combination C-1	Combination C-3	
		OR	
Blood Purifier	Yellow Dock Root	Licorice Root	Blood Purifier
	Dandelion Root	Red Clover Tops	
	Burdock Root	Sarsaparilla Root	
	Licorice Root	Cascara Sagrada Bark	
	Chaparral Herb	Oregon Grape Root	
	Red Clover Tops	Chaparral Herb	
	Barberry Rootbark	Burdock Root	
	Cascara Sagrada Bark	Buckthorn Bark	
	Yarrow Herb	Prickly Ash Bark	
	Sarsaparilla Root	Peach Bark	
		Stillingia Root	

And of course, **when in doubt, clean out.** I'd start with my bowel and run through the rest of my organs in turn.

One thing I'd always work on, no matter what the reason for high blood pressure, is my nervous system. You would be surprised at how many people tell me, "Oh, my dear, I'm a very calm person. Nothing bothers me. Stress has nothing to do with my high blood pressure." Invariably this is the person who holds everything inside...the "nice lady" down the block who wakes in the night and methodically axes her husband to bits. I'd definitely add a nervine combination or even two:

	Combination B-1	Combination B-17	
		OR	
Herbal Calcium	Comfrey Root	Black Cohosh Root	Nerve Repair
	Alfalfa Herb	Capsicum Fruit	
	Oat Straw	Valerian Root	
	Irish Moss Plant	Mistletoe Herb	
	Horsetail Herb	Lady's Slipper Root	
	Lobelia Herb	Lobelia Herb	
	OR	Skullcap Herb	
		Hops Flowers	
	Combination B-16	Wood Betony Herb	
Nerve Repair	Black Cohosh Root		
	Capsicum Fruit	OR	
	Valerian Root		
	Mistletoe Herb	Combination B-18	
	Ginger Root	Valerian Root	
	St. Johnswort Herb	Anise Seed	Instant Relaxant
	Hops Flowers	Lobelia Herb	
	Wood Betony Herb	Desert Tea (Brigham)	
		Black Walnut Hulls	
		Licorice Root	
		Ginger Root	

Stroke

Let me tell you about a fascinating experience. A naturopathic doctor told me, "Look, when someone seems to be suffering from a stroke, I take *Cayenne Pepper Extract* and rub it on the palms of their hands and the soles of their feet. This equalizes the circulation and brings the blood down from the head. A bit later, I rub *Lobelia Extract* on the palms and soles of the feet. This relaxes the system. Remember this," he entoned, "it works real well."

You know me. I decided to try it. I rushed home and stripped off my long, leather boots and socks. With great deliberation and care, I slathered my palms and the soles of my feet with liquid *Cayenne Pepper*. And waited. Nothing. No heat. No burning sensation. Ah, well. Must have not used enough. Liberally, I applied more to my hands and again to my feet. Maybe if I rubbed just a bit over the soles? Maybe up on the sides a bit? And between the toes? Ummm. Nothing. I sat, with my feet straight out, my toes spread. Maybe a bit more *Cayenne*? Just a little more. Here, let's put some more toward the top of my foot...Still no heat. I sighed. Probably to get the real benefit I needed to rub on the *Lobelia*. I did. Nothing. "Shoot," I muttered to myself. "It sounded like such a good idea." I pulled on my socks and then my boots, stood up and went on with life.

Four hours passed. I was in a fancy restaurant having dinner with Keith and another couple, Betty and Jim. I still wore my boots. They're handsome things and difficult to get off, so I'd simply exchanged a simple blouse for a fancy one and gone out into the night. I was sitting there, eating, talking, laughing. Minding my own business. Can you believe what happened? Suddenly my feet caught fire. The hair on my head must have stood straight up and smoked because Betty said, "For heaven's sake, Venus, what's wrong with you?"

My fork hung in mid-air. I could feel my eyes bulge and stare. I rubbed my feet frantically and quietly along the floor. Betty waited for an answer.

"It's nothing," I said. I figured the fire would burn itself out momentarily. I lifted my toes inside the boots. No relief. The area felt like a brush fire. Maybe if I could pull the boot tops down and let some air in! I took my right foot and tried to push down the left boot. Didn't work. I hunched over and used my hands which brought my chin close to table level. I continued an animated and charming conversation. I yanked on those boots. "Just get them **off**," I begged the universe silently. "And I'll have relief." I pushed and pulled. I grunted. The table shimmied. The waiter stopped by.

"Is everything all right?"

Betty looked under the table. My feet were getting hotter and hotter.

Surely they were blistering and frying in their own juices. "**Why?**" I thought. "Did I give it **three** treatments?"

"Look," I breathed. I pulled myself up from practically under the table. "I have to go to the restroom."

Keith, Betty and Jim watched me. My lovely and expensive French meal sat untouched on my plate.

"Are you in pain?" Jim asked. "You don't look right to me."

"No, no," I mumbled. "It's just these boots."

I didn't have time to give a detailed and amusing explanation. At the moment, it wasn't funny. I untangled my hands from my feet and rushed to the ladies room. Once there, unmindful of the cluster of pearled and silked women I sat down on the floor and yanked at those damn boots. I rolled practically backward trying to get them off. I was now in a frenzy. I was sure my feet were scorched and even streaming fire. I grunted and huffed. There! One boot off. I gave it a toss. Then another! That one flew too. I ripped off my socks and pulled my feet toward my face. I had an attentive audience. In fact, the women were fascinated. "My feet caught fire." I explained. I looked at my feet closely. They looked just the same as they always had. I jumped up and headed for the wash basin. My public swiftly cleared a path. Turning the water on full force I stuck one foot under the tap and then another. I soaped and scrubbed and soaked. Let me tell you. Once *Cayenne* is on you, nothing gets it off.

Eventually the burning sensation quieted enough for me to return to my table and finish dinner. However, that night remains a memorable evening.

I recall the naturopath's words: "Remember this. It works real well."
I remember.

After The Fact

These herbs are traditionally used after a stroke to repair the damage. It takes time.

Gotu Kola: Repairs the brain.

Blessed Thistle: Gets oxygen to the brain and heart.

Skullcap: Works on the medulla and the entire spinal cord.

The *Nervine Herbs* and *Combinations* of the same: These help repair nerve damage.

Continued...

Instant Relaxation	**Combination B-18** Valerian Root Anise Seed Lobelia Herb Desert Tea (Brigham) Black Walnut Hulls Licorice Root Ginger Root	**Combination B-2** Comfrey Root Horsetail (Shavegrass) Herb Oat Straw Lobelia Herb	Tissue Repair
	AND	**Combination B-17** Black Cohosh Root Capsicum Fruit Valerian Root Mistletoe Herb Lady's Slipper Root Lobelia Herb Skullcap Herb Hops Flowers Wood Betony Herb	Repairs Nerve Damage
Tissue Repair	**Combination B-1** Comfrey Root Alfalfa Herb Oat Straw Irish Moss Plant Horsetail Herb Lobelia Herb		
		OR	
		Combination B-16 Black Cohosh Root Capsicum Fruit Valerian Root Mistletoe Herb Ginger Root St. Johnswort Herb Hops Flowers Wood Betony Herb	Repairs Nerve Damage

Circulation—Hot And Cold

Becky knows an 85-year-old man who's never been to a doctor. He says, "Everyday I take a teaspoon of *Capsicum* (same as *Cayenne*) and one whole lemon's juice in water. Keeps my blood moving. For depression and a long life, I take *Capsicum* and *Garlic* and eat *Onions*."

When John gets too hot in the summer time he takes *Capsicum*. He says, "It cools me off and makes me comfortable. I get so hot inside that anything outside feels cool."

Dorothy told me she'd had cold hands and feet for years. "Now that I take *Kelp* they're no longer cold."

For more temperature balance some people take the herbal combinations used to balance the thyroid.[26]

Macho Bob

Would you like to know what I did to Bob? This happened when I was new to herbs. I used to visit my mentor, Henry.[27] I'd sit with him and complain, "I'm so tired, Henry. I have so much to do and I'm just ex-

26. See Appendix I
27. *The Outrageous Herb Lady,* Venus Catherine Andrecht

hausted. I can't even get off the couch. And, I'm cold, too." I'd wrap my little arms around my frail body and look pathetic. One day, Henry sprung into action.

"Hey, hey!" he shouted. He stood and wagged a boney finger at me. "I've got just the right thing! Wait right here!" In a flash he'd disappeared and was back with six *Capsicum* capsules and a glass of water. "Drink!" he hollered.

I did.

Within 15 minutes I found myself lifting off the couch like a fast plane at take-off.

"Boy!" I said. "Got to go. Got work to do!" I flew out of the house without a backward glance. *Capsicum* really worked!

I like to help people. Several weeks later, I got an opportunity. I was then working in real estate. Our office of about 25 agents was quietly humming along. I was busily rearranging papers at my desk when Bob ambled by. "I'm so tired," he said to me. "Can't seem to get anything done."

"I can help you!" I said quickly. I was remembering my experience with Henry and the *Capsicum*.

"Oh no you won't," said Bob. He shook his slicked back head of hair and picked nervously at his watch. "You aren't getting me to take any of your voodoo herbs."

For weeks at the office I'd been plying everyone with herbs, but Bob had been an office hold-out. A happy bachelor of 35, he had a macho image to uphold. "Oh come on Bob," I wheedled. "This is nothing exotic. It's one simple herb." I recounted my success with *Capsicum*.

Bob looked at me with concentration and held out his hand. "All right. Give me some. But they'd better not kill me."

"Oh boy," I said. "You'll really like these."

I dropped six *Capsicum* into his palm. "Just swallow them," I advised. I watched as he walked casually to the water cooler. On his way he cocked his head and winked at one of the secretaries. Such a cool guy.

Fifteen or 20 minutes passed. I was engrossed in paperwork. Suddenly, Bob flew up to my desk. The force of his appearance blew my papers to the floor. "Mr. Cool" clutched his stomach.

"Gawd," he hissed. "I'm dying. Honest to gawd, I'm dying!" I looked at him with alarm. "My stomach's on fire!" he practically cried. He started to pace. His voice raised a few octaves. "What the hell did you give me?" Sweat ran down his face as he turned to several of the other agents. "I'm on fire!" His carefully cultivated image fell away. He doubled over and moaned.

"Oh come on Bob," I said. "You're not dying. *Capsicum* is just hot. That's what gives you the energy."

"Hot, hell!" Bob wailed.

"Listen," I said. "Did you take it with food on your stomach?"

"No," Bob said shortly. "I took it with water."

"OK, that's good," I replied. "How much water?"

Bob gave me a scathing look. "A few swallows."

"Well, that's it," I said reasonably. "You didn't drink enough water and you should have had food in your stomach. Now, if we had tomato juice, some salad oil or some raw parsley, that burning sensation would go right away."

"So great," Bob cut in. "I just don't carry raw parsley in my purse!"

"At any rate," I finished. "The *Capsicum* isn't hurting you, really. You just think so."

Bob spent the rest of his *Capsicum* induced energy at the water cooler. I thought he was being a real baby but he refused to ever let me advise him, again.

Traditional Herbs For Circulation

OR

Single Herbs:
Capsicum (Cayenne)
Kelp

Combination BC-18
Hawthorn Berries
Capsicum Fruit
Garlic Bulb

Combination BC-20
Garlic Bulb
Capsicum Fruit
Parsley Root
Ginger Root
Siberian Ginseng Root
Golden Seal Root

The Herbs For Thyroid Balance

Used by people who are **cold** due to thyroid imbalance.

OR

Combination B-19
Kelp Plant
Irish Moss Plant
Parsley Herb
Capsicum Fruit

Combination B-20
Irish Moss Plant
Kelp Plant
Black Walnut Hulls
Parsley Herb
Watercress Herb
Sarsaparilla Root
Iceland Moss Plant

Hemorrhoids

Sometimes you have hemorrhoids before you start a cleanse. Sometimes after. It depends on how hard you cleanse. If you develop them **after** an herb program, you may have had them all along. They were just tucked up inside minding their own business. Either way, they can be very uncomfortable. Here's the way one woman dealt with them:

Harriet's Hemorrhoidectomy

Harriet is fat. Really fat! Put four people together and tie them with a rubber band and that's Harriet. But she's healthy and good-natured and will try anything.

She came to see me one day with her chubby two year old, Danny. He raced around the room while I said, "Hi, sit down."

Harriet chose the couch. We exchanged a few "Hi, how are you? I'm fines." She yelled at Danny several times, "Hey, kid, stop squeezing oranges through Venus' window screens!" Then she swooped into the topic at hand.

"Well," she pronounced in her throaty voice. "I have a problem. Ahaha, hahah!" She clapped her hands together. "I have hemorrhoids. I have to tell you, ahahahah!...It's time to get rid of them," she continued. "I've decided to use some herbs. My neighbor told me she used *White Oat Bark, Goldenseal* and *Cayenne Pepper.* She took them internally everyday, plus..." she paused dramatically, "she made a paste out of them...you know, mixed them with water or *Aloe Vera Gel.*" Her voice dropped, "And then inserted them up her bum several times a day."

She looked at me with satisfaction. "Those piles went away. Can you believe it? It took three to four weeks, Venus, but they went **away!** Ahaha hah!"

"Sure," I said. "I've seen it happen a lot. You're going to try it?"

"Yes," Harriet said shaking her body affirmatively. "I just came to get those herbs."

"OK," I agreed. "However, let me caution you. If I were mixing up *Goldenseal, White Oak Bark* and *Cayenne Pepper,*[28] I'd be extremely careful about the amount of *Cayenne Pepper. Cayenne Pepper* is **very, very** hot. It stops bleeding and brings circulation into an area. That's why it's used in that formula. But really, Harriet, go **easy** on the amount. I'd use one capsule each of the *Goldenseal* and *White Oak Bark,* but only **one-eighth** of a capsule of *Cayenne Pepper.* It won't hurt

28. *Capsicum*

115

you, but too much would be uncomfortable. You hear what I said?"

"Sure," Harriet boomed. "Sounds like fun. Let's get those herbs and get out of here. Son! Stop squeezing those oranges through Venus' screens."

Several days later I got a phone call.

"Wowee Willie!" the caller yelled. "This is Harriet! Wowee! Wait till I tell you what happened to me!... Well!" I could picture her settling into a chair for a serious discussion. "Well, I mixed those herbs up. You know, poured out some *Goldenseal,* right? Poured in some *White Oak Bark...*Poured in a little *Cayenne Pepper.* Then I mixed it up with *Aloe Vera Gel,* see...? Well, I looked at that stuff and I thought, 'I'm bigger than most people,' right? I need more *Cayenne Pepper.* So, that's what I did. Poured in more. Well!" she heaved a big sigh. "I inserted that stuff up my rear end just like my neighbor said...And I'd like to **tell** you! Well!" she let out a screech. "I caught fire! Ahahahah! ha ha! I mean, Venus, I think there were flames shooting out my back side. I screamed and started running through the house. This upset Danny and he started screaming and running after me!"

I could see it. Huge Harriet racing through her house at top speed with her little kid right behind her.

"Well," she continued. "I ran to the bathroom, drew water in the sink and put my rear in. Sink was too small. I hopped out and ran to the kitchen. Sat in that sink. Size was OK, but it was full of dishes and sharp forks. Jumped out of that one and hollered my way into the bathtub. That fit OK, it just didn't help. It must have took me an hour to put out the flames!"

"Gee," I said. "What an experience."

"You bet," Harriet agreed. "But everything worked out OK, that's why I called. No more hemorrhoids! One treatment did the job!"

Harriet's Hemorrhoid Special

White Oak Bark: Traditionally shrinks things. She took six capsules.

Goldenseal: Historically kills infections. Harriet took three.

Cayenne Pepper: She took three capsules.

...And you know how she took the suppository.

For the Suppository: I would have mixed one capsule of *White Oak Bark* with one capsule of *Goldenseal* and **one-eighth** of a capsule of *Cayenne Pepper.*

Prostate Problems

The prostate. Most men have trouble with this. Even young men. And they worry about it. Sometimes the problem is caused by worms in the tubing, sometimes not. Here's a program many men use:

Traditionally cleans the bowel and kills worms

Combination C-5
Pumpkin Seeds
Culver's Root
Mandrake Root
Violet Leaves
Comfrey Root
Cascara Sagrada Bark
Witch Hazel Bark
Mullein Leaves
Slippery Elm Bark

PLUS

Bee Pollen: This has many nutrients

AND

Zinc = Sex

AND

Prostate Flushers

Combination BC-13
Black Cohosh Root
Licorice Root
Kelp Plant
Gotu Kola Herb
Golden Seal Root
Capsicum Fruit
Ginger Root
Lobelia Herb

OR

Combination BC-12
Juniper Berries
Goldenseal Root
Capsicum Fruit
Parsley Herb
Ginger Root
Siberian Ginseng Root
Uva Ursi Leaves

Prostate Flushers

Pumpkin Seeds and *Black Walnut* historically kill worms.

PLUS

Combination C-4
Gentian Root
Irish Moss Plant
Golden Seal Root
Comfrey Root
Fenugreek Seeds
Mandrake Root
Safflower Flowers
Myrrh Gum
Yellow Dock Root

Echinacea Root
Black Walnut Hulls
Barberry Rootbark
Dandelion Root
St. Johnswort Herb
Chickweed Herb
Catnip Herb
Cyani (Cornflower) Flowers

Combination C-4 is a traditional cell cleanser. Some men take it, along with the prostate herbs. Like anything else, this prostate program needs patience and at least six months.

She Cures Her Man

While lecturing in Canada, I met an older lady who told me the herbs had cured her husband of prostate cancer. She gave him the regular herbs for the prostate, but added an extra. She had noticed that doctors give men with prostate cancer, estrogen, the female hormone, to control the cancer. She reasoned, "These men must have too many male hormones which may lead to that particular cancer...so, why not give the herbal **female** hormones? She did and the doctors say her husband is cured. He took the prostate herbs, *Combination C-4* and:

Combination B-5
Golden Seal Root
Red Raspberry Leaves
Black Cohosh Root
Queen of the Meadow Herb   Herbal
Marshmallow Root   Hormones
Blessed Thistle Herb
Lobelia Herb
Capsicum Fruit
Ginger Root

OR

Combination B-8   Herbal
Golden Seal Root   Hormones
Red Raspberry Leaves   Same as **Combination
Black Cohosh Root   B-5**, but with
Queen of the Meadow Herb   *Dong Quoi* added.
Marshmallow Root
Blessed Thistle Herb
Lobelia Herb
Capsicum Fruit
Ginger Root
Dong Quoi

Alternated with:

Combination B-6
Golden Seal Root
Capsicum Fruit
False Unicorn Root
Ginger Root   Herbal
Uva Ursi Leaves   Hormones
Cramp Bark
Squaw Vine Herb
Blessed Thistle Herb
Red Raspberry Leaves

She also threw in some *Black Cohosh* and sometimes *Dong Quoi*. Don't be alarmed if a man passes blood while on this program. The toxins have to come out.

The Perfect Pair

Some friends of mine had a few problems. Their daughter was 19 and had never menstruated. The family was becoming alarmed and the girl herself was wondering and worrying. Meanwhile, the father had a stubborn prostate problem and needed relief. A program was carefully chosen. The father put himself on all the prostate herbs and the daughter took female hormone herbs. Five or six months went by and the happy call came. Dad was doing much better and Bernice had started her period.

A week or two later, they both came in my office, beaming. "We're here for refills on those terrific herbs. I feel so much better!" 'Dad' said. Carefully, I bagged 'Dad's' herbs. Then bagged Bernice's and handed them over. "Oh, here," Bernice said. "You've got them switched." I watched in fascination as they exchanged bags.

"Yep," said 'Dad,' "Here's my *Black Cohosh, Dong Quoi* and all the rest of 'em." I sat. **Fawamp!**, in my chair. All these months the father had taken women's herbs and Bernice had taken her Dad's prostate regulators.

I snuck a look as 'Dad' retreated out the door. He looked as male as ever and I saw no hair on Bernice's chest.

It was a new one on me.

Terminal Diseases

Linda's uncle, "was sent home from the hospital by his doctor, 'to die.' Instead," Linda told me, "he took *Capsicum, Garlic* and a good *Protein Powder.* He's now out mowing his lawn."

Just because someone tells you you're going to die doesn't mean you have to do it. I've known scores of people who thought they were facing the Pearly Gates. They were packed and ready to go, even had their train reservations. For many, the trip was canceled. My axiom applies here: **When in doubt, clean 'em out.** Often a good cleanse will move so many poisons that the body will heal itself. I'd certainly start with a good bowel cleanse.[29] And move into a blood cleanse.[30] Then I'd read up on all the herbs and vitamins that are generally used for my particular problem. I'd put myself on a program and most important, I'd stay on it.

Lumps And Bumps

Lumps and bumps scare most people. They scare me. But, I've known lots of people and animals who've recovered, permanently, using natural methods.

The first thing I'd do is go on the *Comfrey-Pepsin Cleanse.* To this I'd definitely add *Pau d'Arco.* This is a tree bark. It historically kills cancers, virus, bacteria and fungus. Good results have also been reported with M.S., diabetes, leukemia, kidneys, liver, varicose veins, etc. I'd add *Chaparral* (often used with melanomas) and *Red Clover Tops* which have a reputation as a blood purifier. I'd probably add in a super-duper combination of herbs used as a blood cleanser,[31] too. I'd remember to add some *Building Herbs* and *Vitamins.* My diet would be as perfect as possible.

If I Had A Terminal Illness
My Program Would Be:

Single Herbs:
Comfrey-Pepsin Cleanse
Pau d'Arco
Chaparral
Red Clover Tops

AND

Continued...

---

29. See Appendix I
30. See Appendix I
31. See Appendix I

	Combination C-1	OR **Combination C-3**	
Blood Purifier	Yellow Dock Root Dandelion Root Burdock Root Licorice Root Chaparral Herb Red Clover Tops Barberry Rootbark Cascara Sagrada Bark Yarrow Herb Sarsaparilla Root	Licorice Root Red Clover Tops Sarsaparilla Root Cascara Sagrada Bark Oregon Grape Root Chaparral Herb Burdock Root Buckthorn Bark Prickly Ash Bark Peach Bark Stillingia Root	Blood Purifier

PLUS

A Good Vitamin Program
Building Herbs
A Good Diet

Later, I might add a combination of herbs that historically clean the cells and kill parasites:

	Combination C-4	OR **Combination C-5**	
Cell Cleanser	Gentian Root Irish Moss Plant Golden Seal Root Comfrey Root Fenugreek Seeds Mandrake Root Safflower Flowers Myrrh Gum Yellow Dock Root Echinacea Root Black Walnut Hulls Barberry Rootbark Dandelion Rootbark St. Johswort Herb Chickweed Herb Catnip Herb Cyani (Cornflower) Flowers	Pumpkin Seeds Culver's Root Mandrake Root Violet Leaves Comfrey Root Cascara Sagrada Bark Witch Hazel Bark Mullein Leaves Slippery Elm Bark	Bowel Cleanser, Worm Killer

Happy Reports

Here's a note from a lady I never met. She's referring to her 4-year-old son who has leukemia. "Since we have started him on *Chaparral* and *Red Clover Tops, Pau d'Arco* and *Vitamin C Powder,* his immunity level and blood level have been in the high range. His energy has been wonderful and coloring and all is beautiful. If all this continues so well with him, it will be a miracle."

Another woman says, "My doctor gave up on me. On a scale of one to ten with this cancer, the pain was ten plus, plus. A few weeks of taking *Pau d'Arco* and the pain is down to one."

A man with leukemia. "I'd tried everything. I was having transfusions all the time. When my wife went to the grocery store she never knew if she'd come home and find me dead. Then I began taking *Pau d'Arco*. I've taken it for a month now. I've lost my gray color and look pink and vibrant. I feel and look to be in perfect health."

Another man's wife reports. "Harry was terminal. He was set to die in three weeks. He took *Pau d'Arco*. I just had him to the doctor and they did blood tests and a CAT Scan on him. No cancer."

One lady says, "I had a lump on my rectum. I didn't go to the doctor because I was afraid he'd cut my rear-end off. Instead I drank a lot of *Aloe Vera Juice* and the lump left.

Vicki had a large lump in her uterus. She's using the *Vaginal Suppository*[32] and says the "whatever" is almost gone.

Patty spends a lot of time in the sun. From this she has numerous skin cancers. She says, "I just smear on a *Chinese Herbal Oil*, take lots of *Vitamin A* and *Potassium* and they seem to go away. (Other folks add *Pau d'Arco*.)

I can't vouch for this one, but, I read somewhere that if you drink a *Mint* tea daily you shouldn't get infections or cancers. (No matter what, it'll settle your stomach and sweeten your breath.)

32. See Appendix I

PART VI

Herbs Traditionally Used For All Those Miscellaneous Problems

"There is still an immense amount to be learned about health, but if what is at present known to the few were part of the general knowledge, the average expectation of life could probably be increased by about ten years."

J.B.S. Haldane

Fat

Some People Are Just Too Human

Lupe, my very semi-housekeeper, is a lovely Mexican lady who calls me "Benus." I love Lupe, not because she does such a beautiful job of keeping house for me, but because she keeps me entertained.

One day, mistakingly believing she was dying of some terminal disease, she got drunk on my brandy and spent three hours dying under my bed. Not until I called her doctor and found out the trivial nature of her problem, was I able to coax her out.

This is the same Lupe who stirred up a glass of cleansing powder, left the room for a moment, came back and thoughtlessly drank it. That's Lupe. If you read my first book, *The Outrageous Herb Lady,* you surely remember Lupe. Well, she's confounded me again.

She'd been complaining, "I'm so fat, Benus. You must have something to get rid of my fat." She'd been dusting and rifling through my bottles of herbs. "Look!" She commanded. She gave her underarm a hefty thwack. The flesh swung wildly. She sent me a piteous dog-eyed look.

"OK," I agreed. "Would you like to try some *Glucomannan?* It's a powdered root from China. It swells up in the stomach and makes a person feel full so they don't eat as much. Voila! They lose weight."

Lupe nodded her head. "Oh, Benus," she whined. "Anything."

"It has to be **this** *Glucomannan,*" I said. "I've tested lots of brands and **they** don't swell up. Then you have to follow my instructions or it won't work."

Lupe jiggled her fat nervously as I continued. "I'd take two capsules one-half hour before each meal and I'd take it with a **hot** beverage. See, you have to make sure it swells up in your stomach, or you don't feel full. And if you don't feel full, you'll eat a lot. Right?"

"OK, Benus," Lupe agreed. I handed her the bottle.

"Remember," I repeated. "Two capsules one-half hour before meals with a **hot** beverage."

Two weeks later I got a call. "Benus?"

"Yes, Lupe?"

"My liver hurts." She snuffled a bit into the phone.

"Your liver hurts?" I repeated.

Lupe's voice rose, tinkling near panic. "Could it be the *Glucomannan?*" (Lupe is one of my *Certified Hypochondriacs*) "I can't imagine that it would be," I answered. "All it does is produce bulk that slips right out of your body without doing anything. Lupe..." I began to feel

124

suspicious, I guess because I know Lupe pretty well. "**How** are you taking that stuff?"

"Just like you told me," Lupe said quickly. "Four with each meal, with a hot drink."

"What!" I yelled. "Four? **With** your meals? Are you crazy?" (I guess it's not tact that keeps people coming back to me.) "My gawd, Lupe..." Then I began to laugh. I could picture her sitting down to a two ton plate of tomatoes, rice, beans, salad and fruitcake, and half-way through swallowing four *Glucomannan* and a cup of tea. At the end of her regular meal, the *Glucomannan* would suddenly explode and she'd have the equivalent of two footballs in her stomach pushing on her liver. No wonder it hurt.

Fat Anna From Alabama

Fat Anna from Alabama bounded into my office. "Two hundred one and a quarter pounds!" she yelled. "I've lost six and a quarter pounds in one week! I feel wonderful!" She bounced up and down on her toes. "I could climb mountains." This from a lady who laughed at herbs a week earlier. "And," she beamed. "Other things are happening too. In the mornings, I always had so much mucus in my eyes, I had to wash my face before I could see myself." She gave a body twirl. "I feel fabulous,, not drained, or anything."

Anna was a fast reactor. Most people lose weight more slowly. First their clothes start fitting differently, then gradually, the pounds start slipping away. Results don't always show with the first set of bottles they lug home. A number of people who come to my herb shop, drag in with devasting and even terminal diseases. And what do they want?

"Forget about my other problems," they command. "I want to lose weight."

Fortunately for them, most of the herbs associated with weight loss, also cleanse and help the body repair itself.

Fat folk are difficult. One person may lose weight easily. Others, using the same herbs and diet will sit and cry huge tears, "I can't lose weight. I'm doing the same thing as Nancie Jean and I can't lose weight!"

I believe them. Some people retain water. Their flesh seems to suck it out of the air. They should add the herbs historically used to prevent water retention and help the kidneys, to their anti-fat program. Herbs like:

Anti-fat Herbs

Single Herbs:
Peach Bark
Parsley
Juniper   Useful with water retention.
Dandelion
Uva Ursi

Sometimes they add herbs for the kidneys like:

Combination BC-23   OR
Golden Seal Root
Juniper Berries   **Combination BC-22**
Uva Ursi Leaves   Juniper Berries
Parsley Herb   Parsley Herb
Ginger Root   Uva Ursi Leaves
Marshmallow Root   Dandelion Root
Lobelia Herb   Chamomile Flowers

Others say they've had their thyroid checked and it's fine. However, when they add an *Herbal Thyroid Formula* the weight starts melting off:

                    OR

Combination B-19   **Combination B-20**
Kelp Plant   Irish Moss Plant   Thyroid
Irish Moss Plant   Kelp Plant   Formulas
Parsley Herb   Black Walnut Hulls
Capsicum Fruit   Parsley Herb
                    Watercress Herb
                    Sarsaparilla Root
                    Iceland Moss Plant

Once a person decides to go on a fat program (actually any herb program) they find it quite helpful to muscle test for the herbs they need and the amounts most useful for them. (Refer back to the chapter on *Muscle Testing.*) One lady complained that a sloppy-fat-formula wasn't working for her. She had a friend test her and found she needed 56 of the capsules a day to start the fat rolling. We were all shocked. But it worked. Now she's down to 12 capsules a day and losing weight. (Personally, I wouldn't start with 56. I'd start with a few and work up to that amount. I'd recommend that, unless, of course, you like the way your bathroom is decorated and wouldn't mind spending your life there.)

Fat Anna's Fat Fighters

Combination C-15
Chickweed Herb
Mandrake Root
Licorice Root
Safflower Flowers
Echinacea Root
Black Walnut Hulls
Gotu Kola Herb
Hawthorn Berries
Papaya Fruit
Fennel Seeds
Dandelion Root

These herbs are traditionally used for sloppy fat. Careful. They can keep you on the pot longer than you had planned. Anna took this combination 20 to 30 minutes before each meal to help cut her appetite.

Single Herbs:
Peach Bark
Parsley
Juniper
Dandelion
Uva Ursi

These herbs are traditionally used to prevent water retention. Anna choose two.

Chickweed

Has a reputation as a fat eater.

Glucomannan

Swells in the stomach causing a full feeling.

Combination B-19
Kelp Plant
Irish Moss Plant
Parsley Herb
Capsicum Fruit

Combination B-19 and **Combination B-20** are often used to balance the thyroid. Anna used them alternately.

OR

Combination B-20
Irish Moss Plant   *Watercress Herb*
Kelp Plant   *Sarsaparilla Root*
Black Walnut Hulls   *Iceland Moss Plant*
Parsley Herb

Licorice Root

Anna took this one because she felt it kept her blood sugar up, relieving fatigue and depression. Go easy on it if you have high blood pressure.

Combination B-35
Fennel
Hawthorn
Licorice Root

Many people use this combination three or four times a day if they're losing weight the tough way; fasting. These herbs traditionally support the adrenals and heart and help you feel better.

Some people find *Don's Liver-Gallbladder Flush* very helpful when trying to lose weight. And, of course, there's my favorite, the *Comfrey-Pepsin Cleanse.* I would just add a few of Anna's anti-fat herbs and combinations to that cleanse.

Ex-Fat Lady

A friend of mine was indignant. "I know a lady who bounces regularly, an hour a day, or two, on a small trampoline. She's lost 40 pounds! She went from a size 18 dress to a size 7! She also went from a 34C bra to a 34DD! She used to complain all the time, had a bad knee and high blood pressure. All those things are gone now." My friend stopped for breath and then huffed, "The thing is, she eats more than any man. She eats and drinks like a pig!"

Yes. It's hard to be so pure while you struggle to lose weight and see someone do it easily by bouncing and singing crazily on a trampoline. But, this example says a lot about exercise. Do it. Along with the herbs and less food, you've got to succeed.

Addictions

Smoking, Speed, Coffee, Alcohol, etc.

These pleasant vices are hard to kick because nicotine, caffeine, alcohol and drugs get into the blood stream and keep you craving for more. I know several ladies who are hooked on speed. One has three small children, a huge splashy house, two acres and a husband who expects and demands that she keep everything neat and cared for. She does. She's speeded every day of her life and he hasn't noticed it yet. She doesn't want to quit, "How would I get everything done that he expects me to do?"

Another, a hair dresser, easily quit with the *Anti-Smoking Formula.* This formula was put together by a nameless man who called it his *Fool-Proof Stop Smoking Program:*

Anti-Smoking Or Anti-Anything

Combinations for Nerve Repair: To quiet the urge to smoke, or whatever:

OR

Combination B-15
Valerian Root
Scullcap Herb
Hops Flowers

OR

Combination B-16
Black Cohosh Root
Capsicum Fruit
Valerian Root
Mistletoe Herb
Ginger Root
St. Johnswort Herb
Hops Flowers
Wood Betony Herb

Combination B-17
Black Cohosh Root
Capsicum Fruit
Valerian Root
Mistletoe Herb
Lady's Slipper Root
Lobelia Herb
Scullcap Herb
Hops Flowers
Wood Betony Herb

A *Deep-lung Cleansing Combination:*   To clean nicotine and mucus from the lungs.

OR   AND

Combination C-16
Comfrey Root
Marshmallow Root
Mullein Leaves
Slippery Elm Bark
Lobelia Herb

Combination C-17
Comfrey Root
Marshmallow Root
Lobelia Herb
Chickweed Herb
Mullein Leaves

Combination C-18
Comfrey Root
Fenugreek Seeds

Continued...

Licorice Root: To support adrenals and keep blood sugar up.

A *Blood Purifying Combination:* To clear the system of nicotine, alcohol or drugs.

Combination C1
Yellow Dock Root
Dandelion Root
Burdock Root
Licorice Root
Chaparral Herb
Red Clover Tops
Barberry Rootbark
Cascara Sagrada Bark
Yarrow Herb
Sarsaparilla Root

OR

Combination C-2
Red Clover Tops
Chaparral
Secret Herb

OR

Combination C-3
Licorice Root
Red Clover Tops
Sarsaparilla Root
Cascara Sagrada Bark
Oregon Grape Root
Chaparral Herb
Burdock Root
Buckthorn Bark
Prickly Ash Bark
Peach Bark
Stillingia Root

Chewable Vitamin C: As a substitution. It's something to put in the mouth, plus smoking destroys *Vitamin C.*

Chamomile Flowers: Traditionally used for drug withdrawal. Soothing.

Catnip and *Fennel:* For tobacco craving.

Combination C-4
Gentian Root
Irish Moss Plant
Golden Seal Root
Comfrey Root
Fenugreek Seeds
Mandrake Root
Safflower Flowers
Myrrh Gum
Yellow Dock Root
Echinacea Root
Black Walnut Hulls
Barberry Rootbark
Dandelion Root
St. Johnswort Herb
Chickweed Herb
Catnip Herb
Cyani (Cornflower) Flowers

This is reputed to be a deep cell cleanser.

Continued...

A Good Bowel Cleanser

Combination C-5	OR	OR
Pumpkin Seeds		
Culver's Root	**Combination C-6**	**Combination C-7**
Mandrake Root	Cascara Sagrada Bark	Cascara Sagrada Bark
Violet Leaves	Buckthorn Bark	Rhubarb Root
Comfrey Root	Licorice Root	Golden Seal Root
Cascara Sagrada Bark	Capsicum Fruit	Capsicum Fruit
Witch Hazel Bark	Ginger Root	Ginger Root
Mullein Leaves	Barberry Rootbark	Barberry Rootbark
Slippery Elm Bark	Couch-grass Herb	Lobelia Herb
	Red Clover Tops	Fennel Seeds
	Lobelia Herb	Red Raspberry Leaves

The man who related this was a heavy smoker and says the program worked for him. With all this, who would have time to smoke?

Alcoholics

Alcoholics use a similar program adding:

Golden Seal Root

and

Dandelion

Dropping the lung cleanser.
For a pick-up, they'll often use a combination for energy, like:

Combination B-10
Capsicum Fruit
Siberian Ginseng Root
Gotu Kola Herb

Aloe Vera Juice: Has a reputation for overcoming the craving for alcohol, sugar and nicotine.

One lady told me her husband used to drink three six packs of beer each evening. She thought this was excessive and started slipping *Aloe Vera* into his apple juice. "Now," she says. "He's down to one six pack and hasn't even noticed the difference."

With any type of addiction, the person needs to work with the herbs willingly. You can't drag someone to it kicking and screaming and expect good results.

If you insist on your vice, here's a few ideas for hangovers.

Hangovers

Amy says this is her answer: Two to four capsules of the instant energy combination:

Combination B-10
Capsicum Fruit
Siberian Ginseng Root
Gotu Kola Herb

AND

one teaspoon of *Siberian Ginseng,* liquid.

Richard has a more novel idea. He and his hangover settle in to watch Sunday morning football. He slumps down in his chair, with an old diaper tied around his forehead, loaded with sliced potatoes.

Energy And Well Being

Years ago, I belonged to a group that believed something like this: "Keep your thoughts on a high level, keep your eyes and mind on spiritual things. Meditate. Let the crazy lowlife world do it's thing while you remain apart and pure. Your body will take care of itself, because your mind is so clean and high." This group would sit around, discuss mind-clearing, meditate, nod, smile graciously, go without food all day, drink gallons of cokes and coffee and smoke like crazy folk until 2 a.m. every morning. They'd go for days on end like this. After several years, I began to tire. Physically and mentally. One night I was at **another** 2 a.m.er. I looked around me. We all sat, schrunched up on metal chairs in a tiny room discussing some lofty topic. My friends were smoking and downing cokes. I could barely see their pinched and pale little faces through the clouds of nauseating smoke. For all their platitudes, nobody looked healthy to me. The bell of sanity rang in my ears: Balance in all things.

A healthy mind has a lot of trouble in a sick body. It's much harder to be uplifted, logical, spiritual, heavenly and loving if you feel like hell.

33 Year Old In 70 Year Old's Body

Here's Dale's story. "When I met you, Venus, I felt like I was going to die. I felt barely conscious. I had a racing heart, hyper-ventilated all the time and was exhausted. I felt **awful**. And I'm only 33. My cholesterol and blood pressure were also dangerously high. The first doctor I went to said it was all in my head. The second doctor said it would all go away if I lost weight. (I did and it didn't.) Then I started taking herbs for my heart: *Hawthorn* and a *Calcium Combination*. After about three months I was still real nervous about my heart so I went and saw a top cardiologist. I'm 33, remember, but he told me I had the body of a 70 year old!! Except for my heart...which was in great shape! Later, I sat down and thought, 'This is really odd. The only thing I've got going for me is my heart and I've been taking herbs for that.' If I hadn't been...well. You know the rest of the story. I put myself on a great herbal program to clean out and build up and today I'm a new man. I feel wonderful! I tell everybody. I tell ya'...I'm a happy man! "

My Son The Star

I received a letter. "I can't tell you how I felt when **my** son was the one who repeatedly shot out and saved the team, over and over! He's taking those energy herbs. He's so impressed that he even keeps an herb book in his locker at school."

My Son The Stars' Secret

Combination B-9
Siberian Ginseng Rootbark
Ho Shou-Wu Root
Black Walnut Hulls
Licorice Root
Gentian Root   Builds
Comfrey Root   Energy
Fennel Seeds
Bee Pollen
Bayberry Rootbark
Myrrh Gum
Peppermint Leaves
Safflower Flowers
Eucalyptus Leaves
Lemongrass Herb
Capsicum Fruit

Harvey, about 70, came up to me after class. He gave me a little nudge and a grin. "Heh heh. I'm taking that *Fast Energy* combo. I take it right before I go bowling...heh, heh. I always get the   best score, now. The guys can't figure what's come over me."

"That's terrific," I applauded. "Why don't you tell the other guys about it?"

"Are you kidding," Harvey answered. "I like being the best."

Harvey's Secret

Combination B-10
Capsicum Fruit   Instant
Siberian Ginseng Root   Energy
Gotu Kola Herb

Judy B. told me, "When I was taking *Alfalfa* that was the best I ever felt in my life!" Well, Judy?...

Animals

Edgar Never Sees Heaven

My brother, Jim, called one evening. "Edgar's sick." Jim's voice trembled. "Which one is Edgar?" I said, sorting through my memory. Jim and his wife, Debbie, generally have about 15 to 20 cats. All favorites.

Jim was shocked. "Oh you know Edgar," he said. "The one Art gave us. The one that cost $250."

"Oh," I replied. "Of course. The one that visits everyone in the neighborhood. The one that sits on the front step of your restaurant, the father of Summer's cat."

"No," Jim said, exasperated. "You're thinking of Fat Cat. This is **Edgar,** Venus."

"OK, Jim, OK, what's wrong with Edgar?"

"Gosh Venus, it's really bad. Edgar has cancer." Jim choked a bit and went on. "They took X-rays and he's got tumors all through him. Clear through his stomach and into his pancreas." Jim stopped a moment to collect himself and then continued. "They cut him open Venus. He's loaded with cancers. They sewed him right up." There was a pause while I mumbled my sorrow. "What can we do?" Jim begged. "We'll do anything to save Edgar."

I posed a stiff question. "Will you give him herbs?"

"Yes," Jim agreed. "Anything."

The next day Jim hot-footed over and picked up some *Pau d'Arco* capsules. The plan was to open one or two and hide them in Edgar's food daily. Jim told me later, "He loves the stuff."

Time passed. Two months later, Edgar visited the vet. X-rays were taken. No tumors. Blood was drawn. No cancer.

"Let's cut him open and look," the vet said.

"No thanks," said Jim. "We know enough."

Almost a year later, Edgar is climbing trees, rolling in dust holes, taking rides in stranger's cars and generally being a regular cat. He's had no more health problems.

Many people already know this: It's best to treat animals like people. Certainly when it comes to herbs, animals react just as well and even better. Their bodies are cleaner, more pure. How many dogs do you know that smoke, drink and sit around and tell dirty stories until three in the morning?

Here's a few true stories just to give you an idea, but, like I said, I think the easiest thing to do is think of them as human beings and treat them accordingly.

Louise's Dribbling Lab

This dog had patches of hair missing and lots of skin itch. According to Louise, he "also had urine dribble." She put *Comfrey* in his food along with the *Woman's Suppository Herbal Combination ("Laura's Special")*. (Just shows you what can happen when you get creative.) She claims he's completely recovered.

The Lumpy-Warty Wagger

Elizabeth says, "As for my dog! He had a sensitive lump the size of an egg on his backbone. Now it's smaller than a marble. I'm giving him:

Yellow Dock: A blood purifier.

Comfrey and *Pepsin:* A healer and cleanser.

Capsicum and *Garlic:* For circulation and infections.

Red Clover and *Chaparral:* More blood purifiers, virus killers.

Combination B-1
Comfrey Root
Alfalfa Herb
Oat Straw   The *Calcium* and *Silicon* herbs.
Irish Moss Plant
Horsetail Herb
Lobelia Herb

She adds, "His warts are almost gone, too."

Robin's Rabbits

Robin says, "I'm pulling my rabbits out of a sickness that the vet says **always** kills them. It's some kind of lung illness. I just give them *Comfrey, Thyme* and *Parsley* plus the liquid combination of:

	Combination C-13	
Infection	*Chickweed*	
Fighter	*Black Cohosh*	"I give myself the same stuff."
	Golden Seal	
	Lobelia	
	Skullcap	
	Brigham Tea	
	Licorice	

Dog Drool

From Colorado, a woman tells me that she has a little Doxie that had a foamy drool from the corners of its mouth. "A friend remarked that in an animal that means heart trouble. So, I got to work. I gave that old dog two bottles of *Hawthorn*. He now acts like a pup. He's also stopped drooling.

Heart

Single Herbs:
Hawthorn
Chlorophyll
Vitamin E
Calcium

Feeds the heart.

Combination B-1
Comfrey Root
Alfalfa Herb
Oat Straw
Irish Moss Plant
Horsetail Herb
Lobelia Herb

Repairs tissue, good *Calcium* source.

Tomi Tiddle's Nerves

Summer and I just moved to the country. Along with us came our cats, Mouser and Tomi Tiddles. Tomi is a huge orange ball of a cat with a long nose and tremendous vitality. He had a bit of trouble adjusting to country life. When the rooster went off at 4 a.m., so did Tomi. He'd bound across my bed, push aside the window curtain and peer out. He'd usually come lip to lip with a peacock or two which caused him to spin backward and roll across my face. Then he'd have to sit and talk about the situation. All night he'd be up-down-up-down-up to the windows, over the table, opened every drawer in the kitchen, fought to get under the covers with me and then told me off. Finally, I'd had it. Now, at bedtime, I squirt seven to nine drops of *Lobelia Extract* into his snack. All of us sleep all night, now.

My Old Cat Mouser

Mouser is almost 17 years old. She's been with me through two marriages, one child, several moves across the country and various career changes. While I was out of the country, just to devil and upset me, she fell on a stick. She never quite recovered from the injury. For months her little hip bones jutted through scruffy, dull fur. She passed blood in her feces, her tongue hung out and she'd sit in any little patch of sun she could find.

I knew we'd come to a desperate pass when she peed in the toaster. One day like any other, I dropped a few slices of bread in the toaster as I began lunch. Instantly, there was a stench so overwhelming and amazing that we had to clear the house. I said, "This is it, Mouser. You too, are going on herbs." I tried buttering herb capsules and sliding them down her throat. Ha! She may have been sick, but she had hidden reserves of strength. Finally, I said, "OK, Mouser. This is it. These herbs go in your food. If you won't eat, you'll starve."

For five or six months now, I've put *Pau d'Arco* (historically kills just about everything and builds the immune system) and *Black Walnut Hulls* (used for worms) in her morning food. In the evening she gets:

The Animal Formula:

Combination B-3
Kelp Plant
Dandelion Root   Full of trace elements.
Alfalfa Herb

What a difference. A few moments ago I watched her outside, running and rolling with a leaf, her black fur glistening in the sun. As a side benefit, Tomi Tiddles, the orange cat, always polishes off the remains of Mouser's meals. Since Mouser's herb program began, a once ratty Tomi has turned into a huge, marvelous ball of a cat.

Candi's Kidney Crisis

Remember Grace, the animal herb lady?[33] She has a tiny, hairy dog named Candi. That dog has a talent. She spends most of her time walking on her front legs with her back legs and rear end straight up in the air. Yes, she's talented but she also used to have a problem. One day Grace came to me, and in her words, said, "That crazy dog had kidney stones. I'd had her operated on once and she died on the table. They got her back but the vet said 'pray she don't ever get stones again, an operation would kill 'er.' Then he charged me $300. Heck fire. The next time she got kidney stones I fixed her myself. I gave her that combination what's supposed to dissolve stones. Then, everyday I put lots of fresh lemon juice in her water. That takes the rough edges off, don't you know, so those stones don't hurt like hell comn' out." Grace snorted and stopped for breath. "Worked just fine. Look at that crazy dog would you!" I looked. There was Candi running around on two legs.

33. *The Outrageous Herb Lady,* Venus Catherine Andrecht

```
┌─────────────────────────────────────────────────────┐
│                                                       │
│          Candi's Kidney Stone Recipe                  │
│                                                       │
│   Lemon Juice                                         │
│                                                       │
│   Combination BC-12        Historically flushes and   │
│   Juniper Berries          repairs the kidneys;       │
│   Golden Seal Root         dissolves stones.          │
│   Capsicum Fruit                                      │
│   Parsley Herb                                        │
│   Ginger Root                                         │
│   Siberian Ginseng Root                               │
│   Uva Ursi Leaves                                     │
│   Queen of the Meadow Root                            │
│      (Gravel Root)                                    │
│   Marshmallow Root                                    │
│                                                       │
└─────────────────────────────────────────────────────┘
```

Before Grace left that day she gave me a few more pointers:

"**Allergies**? I give my dogs the regular people herbs for allergies. Those herbs get rid of red dog ears, too!" And I put *Black Walnut Hull Extract* on **Eczema** from flea bites."

Dog Gone Cough Is Gone

Anne's little dog is getting old. Every once in a while now she gets a coughing spell. Anne gives her two drops of *Lobelia Extract* in one-half cup of warm water and one-half teaspoon of honey. She says it works. However, if I had a stubborn dog who wouldn't sip from a cup, I'd drop it down his throat.

Back From The Dead

Elaine's letter came in the mail a few days ago:

"My dog, Kasha, developed a staph infection in her vagina. The vet said this was a very difficult thing to cure. He gave her strong antibiotics, but the infection spread to her kidneys. She lost control of her bladder. I knew this was really serious and began to prepare myself for the vet wanting to 'put her to sleep.' Then, a miracle. I began giving her a *Blood Purifying Combination*. I took her back to the vet the following week. He tested her and said she was making a remarkable comeback! She was cured within a short time. Recently she broke her toe and required a very heavy bandage around her whole leg. The vet said it would take six weeks to heal. I said, "Oh, I don't think so..." and began giving her a *Calcium* combination of herbs:

```
Combination B1
Alfalfa
Comfrey
Horsetail            A good Calcium source.
Irish Moss
Lobelia
Oat Straw
```

I hoped this would mend the bone. In three weeks she chewed off the bandage and we have not been back to the vet. She is running around like crazy. Hooray for herbs!''

Cat Wreck

Stray cats come to me. I think I must be written up in the Traveling Cat's AAA. Recently, another one showed up. This cat was very pregnant. I carried her around the neighborhood trying to find a good home for "Momma." Then, someone disgustedly pointed out that "Momma," was a guy! Thunderstruck by my mistake, I started working on the poor cat's bloat. I used a good bowel cleanser, *Black Walnut Hulls* for his worms and *Pau d'Arco* to kill everything else and build him up. Then, I realized why I always smelled like cat urine. This guy had a leak! To his food I added a *Kidney* and *Bladder Combination* (**Combination BC-12** or **Combination BC-13**) plus *Marshmallow Root* to soothe his inflamed organs. The poor cat was so hungry he'd eat anything and ate it all. He's now perfectly well. And perfectly happy with his new home. Mine.

Diet

While lecturing in Arizona, I met a lady named Ruth. She begged me to include the following information, and I do, gladly.

Her family consists of her dog, Pupper Burton and her cat, Katsy. Pupper Burton, especially, was a suffering creature with arthritis and itching, oozing sores. Not anymore. Ruth fixed him with herbs and a good diet. Ruth says the first thing you need to do with your animal friends, sick or well, is get them off commercial foods. "Animals get loads of preservatives and colorings in most canned and dry foods. This causes illness just as it does in people."

Here's how Ruth feeds her animals:

"Cut up partially frozen (cuts easier) chicken, fish or turkey livers. (No beef.) Add three eggs, preferably fertile, one cup of Bulgar wheat, some sliced raw carrot, garlic, onion, three tablespoons wheat germ, three tablespoons of brewer's yeast, two teaspoons of olive oil, two teaspoons codliver oil. This amount for every pound of meat or fish. Put in small containers and freeze. When blending, if necessary, add a little liquid. Add herbs to this and put over a good dry dog or cat food."

With a little help, your animals can be healthier than you are.

Why It's Best To Stay Away From The Vet

Our Helen, of *Hairball* fame, puts forth the most compelling reason for treating your animals yourself. She told me:

"I took my dog to the vet for a shot. I was bent over the table trying to hold my dog down while the vet struggled to vaccinate him. Suddenly, the door behind me flew open. Before I realized what was happening, something with four feet and claws landed VAWAAMP!! right on my rear and grabbed a hold. My gawd, Venus, it was a mad cat stuck to my ass! I screamed and jumped right over the table, the dog and the vet. It took the vet and two assistants to hold me down and pry that cat loose.

That's the last time my dog's been to the vet."

In Closing

We have come to the end, my friends.
My parting thoughts are:
Keep it simple. Health **is** simple.

Clean out your body and **build** it up. **Repair** major problems as you go along. Don't fuss and frazzle yourself about "What herbs should I take, how many, or for how long." You can choose almost any herb or herbs and they will help you. They're very gracious and accommodating that way. For "how many," you can use muscle testing or good sense. For "how long," until you're well and then a while longer. Then, stay on a maintenance program.

I wish you WELL.

He who has health has hope; and he who has hope has everything.

Arab Proverb

Venus is available for lectures.
Please write for information:

To Contact Venus write:
c/o Ransom Hill Press
P.O. Box 325
Ramona, Ca. 92065
If you wish a reply, please enclose a stamped,
self-addressed envelope.

Appendix I

The following catagories seem so arbitrary. They are guidelines only, as many herbs seem to slide both ways. That's their charm, I guess.

You may occasionally find that a so-called builder acts as a cleanser for you, or vice-versa. That's **your** charm, I guess.

B = Builders   C = Cleansers   BC = Builders and Cleansers

Builders—Combinations

Used for stress and tissue repair:

Combination B-1
Comfrey Root
Alfalfa Herb
Oat Straw
Irish Moss Plant
Horsetail Herb
Lobelia Herb

Combination B-2
Comfrey Root
Horsetail (Shavegrass) Herb
Oat Straw
Lobelia Herb

Blood builders:

Combination B-3
Kelp Plant
Dandelion Root
Alfalfa Herb

Combination B-4
Red Beet
Yellow Dock
Strawberry Leaves
Lobelia
Burdock Root
Nettle
Mullein Leaves

These are the herbs for women that act like herbal hormones:

Combination B-5
Golden Seal Root
Red Raspberry Leaves
Black Cohosh Root
Queen of the Meadow Herb
Marshmallow Root

Blessed Thistle Herb
Lobelia Herb
Capsicum Fruit
Ginger Root

Combination B-6
Golden Seal Root
Capsicum Fruit
False Unicorn Root
Ginger Root
Uva Ursi Leaves
Cramp Bark
Squaw Vine Herb
Blessed Thistle Herb
Red Raspberry Leaves

Combination B-7
Black Cohosh Root
Licorice Root
False Unicorn Root
Siberian Ginseng Root
Sarsaparilla Root
Squaw Vine Herb
Blessed Thistle Herb

Combination B-8
Golden Seal Root
Dong Quoi
Red Raspberry Leaves
Black Cohosh Root
Queen of the Meadow Herb
Marshmallow Root
Blessed Thistle Herb
Lobelia Herb
Capsicum Fruit
Ginger Root

For energy and to build strength:

Combination B-9
Siberian Ginseng Rootbark
Ho Shou-Wu Root

Black Walnut Hulls
Licorice Root
Gentian Root
Comfrey Root
Fennel Seeds
Bee Pollen
Bayberry Rootbark
Myrrh Gum
Peppermint Leaves
Safflower Flowers
Eucalyptus Leaves
Lemongrass Herb
Capsicum Fruit

Combination B-10
Capsicum Fruit
Siberian Ginseng Root
Gotu Kola Herb

Used by people with low blood sugar problems:

Combination B-11
Licorice Root
Safflower Flowers
Dandelion Root
Horseradish Root

Combination B-12
Soy Protein
Capsicum Fruit
Red Clover Tops

Combination B-13
Peppermint Leaves
Licorice Root
Cinnamon Bark
Spearmint Leaves

Useful with pain:

Combination B-14
Valerian Root
Wild Lettuce Leaves
Capsicum Fruit

To repair the nervous system and relax a person. *Combination B-15* is also used by people who can't sleep, or to relieve pain.

Combination B-15
Valerian Root
Skullcap Herb
Hops Flowers

Combination B-16
Black Cohosh Root
Capsicum Fruit
Valerian Root
Mistletoe Herb
Ginger Root
St. Johnswort Herb
Hops Flowers
Wood Betony Herb

Combination B-17
Black Cohosh Root
Capsicum Fruit
Valerian Root
Mistletoe Herb
Lady's Slipper Root
Lobelia Herb
Skullcap Herb
Hops Flowers
Wood Betony Herb

Combination B-18
Valerian Root
Anise
Lobelia
Ginger Root
Brigham Tea
Black Walnut Hulls
Licorice Root

For thyroid conditions and glandular systems balance:

Combination B-19
Kelp Plant
Irish Moss Plant
Parsley Herb
Capsicum Fruit

Combination B-20
Irish Moss Plant
Kelp Plant
Black Walnut Hulls
Parsley Herb
Watercress Herb
Sarsaparilla Root
Iceland Moss Plant

Women take this five to six weeks before they give birth:

Combination B-21
Black Cohosh Root
Squaw Vine Herb
Lobelia Herb
Pennyroyal Herb
Red Raspberry Leaves

This is taken all through pregnancy:

Combination B-22
Hibiscus
Peppermint
Red Raspberry Leaves
Rose Hips

Builds and repairs the sexual organs:

Combination B-23
Siberian Ginseng Root
Echinacea Root
Saw Palmetto Berries
Gotu Kola Herb
Damiana Leaves
Sarsaparilla Root
Periwinkle Herb
Garlic Bulb
Capsicum Fruit
Chickweed Herb

For digestion:

Combination B-24
Papaya Fruit
Ginger Root
Peppermint Leaves
Wild Yam Root
Fennel Seeds
Lobelia Herb
Spearmint Leaves
Catnip Herb

Combination B-25
Papaya Fruit
Mint

Combination B-26
Alfalfa
Mint

Useful with ulcers and inflamations:

Combination B-27
Comfrey Root
Marshmallow Root

Slippery Elm Bark
Ginger Root
Wild Yam Root
Lobelia Herb

Combination B-28
Golden Seal Root
Capsicum Fruit
Myrrh Gum

For bones, joints, ligaments, cartilage and tissue repair.

Combination B-29
Comfrey Root
Golden Seal Root
Slippery Elm Bark
Aloe Leaves (Resin)

Combination B-30
White Oak Bark
Comfrey Root
Mullein Leaves
Black Walnut Leaves
Marshmallow
Queen of the Meadow
Wormwood Herb
Lobelia
Skullcap

Combination B-31
Comfrey
Dandelion
Ginseng
Wood Betony

Hair, skin, nails and potassium lack:

Combination B-32
Kelp
Dulse
Watercress
Wild Cabbage
Horseradish
Horsetail

Combination B-33
Dulse
Horsetail
Sage
Rosemary

Combination B-34
A Trace Mineral Combination

Great when fasting:

Combination B-35
Licorice Root
Hawthorn
Fennel

Heart and circulation:

Combination B-36
Concentrated Hawthorn
Berries
Vitamin E
Selenium
Apple Pectin

Single builders:
Alfalfa
Bee Pollen
Black Cohosh
Blessed Thistle
Catnip
Blue Cohosh
Damiana
Fennel
Siberian Ginseng
Gotu Kola
Hawthorn
Horsetail
Hops

Kelp
Marshmallow
Oatstraw
Passion Flower
Peppermint
Red Raspberry
Sage
Saw Palmetto
Skullcap
Slippery Elm
Valerian
White Oak Bark
Wood Betony

Cleansers—Combinations

Blood purifiers, often used with skin problems, infections or any disease involved with "dirty" blood:

Combination C-1
Yellow Dock Root
Dandelion Root
Burdock Root
Licorice Root
Chaparral Herb
Red Clover Tops
Barberry Rootbark
Cascara Sagrada Bark
Yarrow Herb
Sarsaparilla Root

Combination C-2
Red Clover Tops
Chaparral
Secret Herb

Combination C-3
Licorice Root
Red Clover Tops
Sarsaparilla Root
Cascara Sagrada
Oregon Grape Root
Chaparral Herb
Burdock Root
Buckthorn Bark
Prickly Ash Bark
Peach Bark
Stillingia Root

Heavy cleansers that also work on parasites and tumors, some people take enemas with them to clear out the loosened toxins:

Combination C-4
Gentian Root
Irish Moss
Golden Seal Root
Comfrey Root
Fenugreek Seeds
Mandrake Root
Safflower Flowers
Myrrh Gum
Yellow Dock Root
Echinacea Root
Black Walnut Hulls
Barberry Rootbark
Dandelion Root
St. Johnswort Herb
Chickweed Herb
Catnip Herb
Cyani (Cornflower)
    Flower

Combination C-5
Pumpkin Seeds
Culver's Root
Mandrake Root
Violet Leaves
Comfrey Root
Cascara Sagrada Bark
Witch Hazel Bark
Mullein Leaves
Slippery Elm Bark

The famous bowel combinations:

Combination C-6
Cascara Sagrada Bark
Buckthorn Bark
Licorice Root
Capsicum Fruit
Ginger Root
Barberry Rootbark

Couch-grass Herb
Red Clover Tops
Lobelia Herb

Combination C-7
Cascara Sagrada Bark
Rhubarb Root
Golden Seal Root
Capsicum Fruit
Ginger Root
Barberry Rootbark
Lobelia Herb
Fennel Seeds
Red Raspberry Leaves

Combination C-8
Comfrey Root
Pepsin

Combination C-9
Psyllium Hulls
Hibiscus Flower
Licorice Root

Infection fighters:

Combination C-10
Echinacea Root
Golden Seal Root
Yarrow Flowers
Capsicum Fruit

Combination C-11
Golden Seal Root
Black Walnut Hulls
Marshmallow Root
Lobelia Herb
Plantain Herb
Bugleweed Herb

Combination C-12
Lobelia Herb
Mullein Leaves

145

Combination C-13
Chickweed
Black Cohosh
Golden Seal Root
Lobelia Herb
Skullcap
Brigham Tea
Licorice

Used by hypoglycemics instead of Combination C-10:

Combination C-14
Echinacea Root
Yarrow Leaves
Myrrh Gum
Capsicum Fruit

A fat fighter and bowel cleanser:

Combination C-15
Chickweed Herb
Mandrake Root
Licorice Root
Safflower Flowers

Echinacea Root
Black Walnut Hulls
Gotu Kola Herb
Hawthorn Berries
Papaya Fruit
Fennel Seeds
Dandelion Root

Deep lung cleansers, also used with allergies:

Combination C-16
Comfrey Root
Marshmallow Root
Mullein Leaves
Slippery Elm Bark
Lobelia Herb

Combination C-17
Comfrey Root
Marshmallow Root
Lobelia Herb
Chickweed Herb
Mullein Leaves

Combination C-18
Comfrey Root
Fenugreek Seeds

Single Cleansers:

Golden Seal
Peach Bark
Psyllium
Red Clover
Redmond Clay
Safflower
Yarrow
Yucca
Aloe Vera
Bayberry
Black Walnut
Buckthorn
Burdock
Chamomile
Cascara Sagrada
Chaparral
Chickweed
Cornsilk

CLEANSERS AND BUILDERS

Arthritis and gout-like conditions:

Combination BC-1
Hydrangea Root
Desert (Brigham) Tea
  Herb
Chaparral Herb
Yucca Root
Black Cohosh Root
Capsicum Fruit
Black Walnut Hulls
Valerian Root
Sarsaparilla Root
Lobelia Herb
Skullcap
Burdock Root
Wild Lettuce Leaves
Wormwood Herb

Combination BC-2
Bromelain
Yucca Root
Comfrey Root
Alfalfa Herb
Black Cohosh Root
Yarrow Flowers
Capsicum Fruit
Chaparral Herb

Lobelia Herb
Burdock Root
Centaury Herb

Liver and gallbladder problems:

Combination BC-3
Red Beet Root
Dandelion Root
Parsley Herb
Horsetail (Shavegrass)
  Herb
Liverwort Herb
Birch Leaves
Lobelia Herb
Blessed Thistle Herb
Angelica Root
Chamomile Flowers
Gentian Root
Golden Rod Herb

Combination BC-4
Barberry Root Bark
Ginger Root
Cramp Bark
Fennel Seeds
Peppermint Leaves
Wild Yam Root

Catnip Herb

To prevent and deal with colds, flus, fevers, diarrhea and vomiting:

Combination BC-5
Bayberry Rootbark
Ginger Root
White Pine Bark
Capsicum Fruit
Cloves Flowers

Combination BC-6
Ginger Root
Capsicum Fruit
Golden Seal Root
Licorice Root

Combination BC-7
Rose Hips
Chamomile Flowers
Slippery Elm Bark
Yarrow Herb
Capsicum Fruit
Golden Seal Root
Myrrh Gum
Peppermint Leaves
Sage Leaves
Lemon-grass Herb

Combination BC-8
Garlic Bulb
Rose Hips
Rosemary Leaves
Parsley Herb

Combination BC-9
Fenugreek Seeds
Thyme Herb

Allergies and sinus conditions:

Combination BC-10
Golden Seal Root
Capsicum Fruit
Parsley Root
Desert (Brigham) Tea
  Herb
Marshmallow Root
Chaparral Herb
Lobelia Herb
Burdock Root

Combination BC-11
Blessed Thistle Herb
Black Cohosh Root
Skullcap
Pleurisy Root

Kidneys, bladder and prostate:

Combination BC-12
Juniper Berries
Golden Seal Root
Capsicum Fruit
Parsley Herb
Ginger Root
Siberian Ginseng Root
Uva Ursi Leaves
Queen of the Meadow Root
  (Gravel Root)
Marshmallow Root

Combination BC-13
Black Cohosh Root
Licorice Root
Kelp Plant
Gotu Kota Herb
Golden Seal Root
Capsicum Fruit
Ginger Root
Lobelia Herb

Eye problems:

Combination BC-14
Golden Seal Root
Bayberry Rootbark
Eyebright Herb

Combination BC-15
Golden Seal Root
Bayberry Rootbark
Eyebright Herb
Red Raspberry Leaves
Capsicum Fruit

Pancreas. Also used by people with diabetes:

Combination BC-16
Golden Seal Root
Juniper Berries
Uva Ursi Leaves
Huckleberry Leaves
Mullein Leaves
Comfrey Root
Yarrow Flowers
Garlic Bulb
Capsicum Fruit
Dandelion Root
Marshmallow Root
Buchu Leaves
Bistort Root
Licorice Root

Combination BC-17
Juniper Berries
Uva Ursi Leaves
Licorice Root
Capsicum Fruit
Mullein Leaves
Golden Seal Root

Circulation and the heart:
Combination BC-18
Hawthorn Berries
Capsicum Fruit
Garlic Bulb

Combination BC-19
Garlic Bulb
Capsicum Fruit

Combination BC-20
Garlic Bulb
Capsicum Fruit
Parsley Root
Ginger Root
Siberian Ginseng Root
Golden Seal Root

Women use this as a vaginal suppository:
Combination BC-21
Squawvine
Chickweed
Slippery Elm
Comfrey

Yellow Dock
Golden Seal Root
Mullein
Marshmallow

Kidney, bladder and other urinary problems:

Combination BC-22
Juniper Berries
Parsley Herb
Uva Ursi Leaves
Dandelion Root
Chamomile Flowers

Combination BC-23
Golden Seal Root
Juniper Berries
Uva Ursi Leaves
Parsley Herb
Ginger Root
Marshmallow Root
Lobelia Herb

SINGLE CLEANSERS AND BUILDERS

Cayenne (Capsicum)
Chlorophyll
Comfrey
Dandelion
Dong Quai
Fenugreek
Garlic
Ginger
Juniper
Licorice
Lobelia
Mullein
Parsley
Rosehips
Sarsaparilla
Pau d'Arco
Uva Ursi
Yellow Dock

147

BIBLIOGRAPHY

Abehsera, Michael, *The Healing Clay*. Swan House Publishing.

Airola, Paavo, Ph.D. N.D. *Every Woman's Book*. Health Plus Publishers, Phoenix, Arizona, 1979

Airola, Paavo, Ph.D. N.D. *The Miracle of Garlic*. Health Plus Publishers, Phoenix, Arizona, 1978

Airola, Paavo, Ph.D. N.D. *How to Get Well*, Health Plus Publishers, Phoenix, Arizina, 1974

Andrecht, Venus, *The Outrageous Herb Lady*. Ransom Hill Press, P.O. box 325, Ramona, Ca. 92065

Max G. Barlow, *From the Shepherd's Purse*. Max Barlow.

Biworld Publishers, *Herb Reference Guide*. 1979 Utah.

Blunt, Wilfred and Raphael, Sandra, *The Illustrated Herbal*. Thames and Hudson, Inc. in association with the Metropolitan Museum of Art. 1979 Great Britain—New York

Bricklin, Mark, *The Practical Encyclopedia of Natural Healing*. Rodale Press, 1976 Pennsylvania, Emmaus

Christopher, John R., Dr., *Childhood Diseases*. Christopher Publications, 1976 Utah

Christopher, John R., Dr., *Capsicum*. Christopher Publications, 1980. Provo, Utah

Christopher, John R., Dr., *Dr. Christopher Talks on Rejuvenation Through Elimination*. Dr. Christopher, 1976. Utah, Provo

Culpeper, Nicholas, *Dr. Culpeper's Herbal Remedies*. Wilshire Book Co., 1971 No. Hollywood, Calif.

Davis, Adelle, *Let's Eat Right To Keep Fit*. Harcourt Brace and World, Inc. 1954 New York

Davis, Adelle, *Let's Get Well.*. Harcourt Brace and Worl, 1965

Davis, Adelle, *Let's Have Healthy Children*. Harcourt Brace and World, Inc., 1951

Diamond, John, M.D., *Your Body Doesn't Lie*. Warner Books, New York, 1979.

Doole, Louise Evans, *Herbs for Health; How To Grow and Use Them*. Wilshire Book Company, 1965 No. Hollywood, Ca.

Fischman, Walter, Dr. and Grinims, Mark Dr. *Muscle Response Test*. Richard Merek, Publishers, New York, 1979.

Gabriel, Ingrid, *Herb Identifier and Handbook*. Sterling Publishing Company, New York, 1977

Gardner, Joy, *Healing Yourself*, Healing Yourself, Seattle, Washington, 1980

Gouzil, Dezirina, *Mother Nature's Herb Teas*, Oliver Press, Willits, California, 1975

Griffin, LaDean, *Health In The Space Age*. BiWorld Publishers, Provo, Utah, 1982

Griffin, LaDean, *Is Any Sick Among You?* BiWorld Publishers, 1974

Griffin, LaDean, *No Side Effects; The Return To Herbal Medicine.* BiWorld Publishers, Provo, Utah, 1975

Griffin, LaDean, *Please Doctor, I'd Rather Do It Myself... With Herbs!* Hawkes Publishing, Inc., 1979

Hanssen, Maurice, *The Healing Power of Pollen.* Thorsons Publishers Limited, Wellingborough, Northamptonshire, 1979.

Harris, Loyd J., *The Book of Garlic.* Aris Books, Berkely, Ca. 1974.

Hatfield, Audrey Wynne, *A Herb For Every Ill.* ST. Martin's Press, New York, 1974

Heinerman, John *Science of Herbal Medicine.* 1979

Heinerman, John, *The Treatment of Cancer With Herbs.* BiWorld Publishers, Orem, Utah, 1980.

Jensen, Bernard, *Health Magic Through Chlorophyll From Living Plant Life.* BiWorld Publishers, Provo, Utah, 1973.

Jensen, Bernard, *Nature Has a Remedy.* Bernard Jensen, 1978.

Jentzsch, Boyd L. and James A. *Ginseng: A Thousand Reasons To Ponder.* Mountain Meadow Enterprises, Salt Lake City, Utah. 1976.

Kapel, Pricilla, *The Body Says Yes.* ACS Publications, San Diego, California 1981

Kerr, Ralph Whiteside, *Herbalism Through The Ages.* Supreme Grand Lodge of Amorc Inc., San Jose, California, 1969.

Klein, Aaron E., *The Parasites We Humans Harbor.* Elsevier/Nelson Books, New York, 1981

Kloss, Jethro, *Back To Eden.* Woodbridge Press Publishing Company, Santa Barbara, California, 1972

Knap, Alyson Hart, *Wild Harvest; An Outdoorsman's Guide to Edible Wild Plants in North America,* Arco Publishing Company, New York, 1975

Kroeger, Hanna, *Ageless Remedies From Mother's Kitchen.* Hanna Kroeger, 1981. Boulder Colorado

Kroeger, Hanna, *Instant Herbal Locator.* Hanna Kroeger, 1979 Boulder, Colorado.

Krutch, Joseph Wood, *Herbal.* David R. Godine, Boston, Massachusetts, 1965.

Law, Donald, *Herb Growing For Health.* ARC Books, New York, 1969

Le Strange, Richard, *A History of Herbal Plants.* Arco Publishing Company, Inc. New York, 1977.

Licata, Vincent. *Comfrey and Chlorophyll.* Continental Health Research, Santa Ana, California, 1969.

Lindberg, Gladys and McGarland, Judy, *Take Charge of Your Health.* Harper and Row Publishers, San Francisco, California, 1982.

Lucas, Richard, *Secrets of the Chinese Herbalists.* Parker Publishing Company, West Nyak, New York, 1977.

Mairesse, Michelle, *Health Secrets of Medicinal Herbs; Medical Benefits and Uses Fully Explained.* ARCO Publishing, Inc., New York, 1981.

Malstrom, Stan, Dr., *Herbal Remedies 2 Revised.* BiWorld Publishers, Orem, Utah, 1975

Malstrom, Stan, Dr., *Natural Herbal Formulas; A Ready-Reference Handbook of the Most Popular Herbal Formulas of Our Day.* Fresh Mountain Air Publishing Company, Orem, Utah, 1977.

McCleod, Dawn, *Herb Handbook; A Practical Guide to Herbs And Their Uses.* Wilshire Book Company, No. Hollywood, California, 1973.

Mendelsohn, Robert S., M.D., *Confessions of a Medical Heretic.* Contemporary Books, Inc., Chicago, Ill. 1979.

Michael, Pamela, *All Good Things Around Us; A Cookbook and Guide to Wild Plants and Herbs.* Holt, Rinehart and Winston, New York, 1980.

Moulton, LeArta, *Herb Walk 1.* The Gluten Company Inc., Provo, Utah, 1979

Murphy, Edith Van Allen, *Indian Uses of Native Plants,* Mendocina County Historical Society, Ft. Bragg, Ca. 1959

Montagna, F. Joseph, *P.D.R. People's Desk Reference; Traditional Herbal Formulas.* Volume I. Quest For Truth Publications, Inc., Lake Oswego, Oregon, 1979.

Montagna, F. Joseph, *P.D.R. People's Desk Reference; Traditional Herbal Formulas,* Volume II, Quest For Truth Publications, Inc., Lake Oswego, Oregon, 1979.

NuLife Publishing, *Provo, Utah, Herbal Combinations From Authoritative Sources.*

Gipsy Petulengro, Romany Remedies And Recipes. Newcastle Publishing Company, Hollywood, California, 1972.

Powell, Eric, F.W. Ph.D., N.D. *Kelp; The Health Giver.* Health Science Press, Hengiscote, Bradford, Holsworthy North Devon, 1968.

The Revolutionary Health Committee of Hunan Province, *A Barefoot Doctor's Manual.* Cloudburst Press, Mayne Isle and Seattle, 1977.

Ritchason, Jack. *The Little Herb Encyclopedia; The Handbook of Nature's Remedies for a Healthier Life.* BiWorld Publishers, Orem, Utah, 1982

Rose, Jeanne, Jeanne Rose's Herbal Guide to Inner Health, Eating the Herbal Way. Grosset and Dunlap, New York, 1979.

Royal, Penny C., *Herbally Yours,* BiWorld, Orem, Utah, 1976

Rudolph Theodore, M. Ph. D., *Chlorophyll, Nature's "Green Magic."* Nutritional Research Publishing Company, San Gabriel, California, 1957.

Salat, Barbara and David Copperfield, Editors, *Well-Being* Anchor Press/Doubleday, Garden City, New York. 1979.

Sanecki, Kay N., *The Complete Book of Herbs.* Mcmillan Publishing Company, Inc., New York, 1974.

Shepard, Stephen Paul, Dr., *Healing Energies.* Hawthorn Books, Provo, Utah, 1981.

Schaeffer, Elizabeth, *Dandelions, Pokeweed and Goosefoot.* Young Scott Books, Reading, Massachusetts, 1972.

Scully, Virginia, *A Treasury of American Indian Herbs.* Crown Publishers, Inc., New York, 1971.

Silverman, Maida, *A City Herbal.* Alfred Knopf, New York, 1977.

Skousen, Max B. *The Ancient Egyptian Plant, Aloe Vera Handbook.* Aloe Vera Research Institute, Lakewood, California, 1979.

Spoerke, David G. Jr. *Herbal Medications.* Woodbridge Press, Santa Barbara, California, 1980.

Stone, Jerry, *Herbal Combinations; Physician's Desk Reference Manual.* Institute Publishers, Huntington Beach, California, 1980.

Stuart, Malcolm, Editor, *The Encyclopedia of Herbs and Herbalism.* Crescent Books, New York, 1979.

Tenney, Louise, *Today's Herbal Health.* Hawthorne Books, Provo, Utah, 1982.

Thie, D.C., *Touch For Health,* DeVorss and Company, Marina Del Rey, California, 1973.

Thomson, Robert, *Natural Medicine.* McGraw Hill Book Company, New York, 1958.

Thornwood Books, *Herb Success Stories; Actual Case Histories.* Thornwood Books, Springville, Utah, 1980.

Tierra, Michael C.A., N.D., *The Way Of Herbs.* Unity Press, Santa Cruz, California 1980.

Troyer, Samuel S.D.C., *Healing With Herbs and Vitamins,* Fresh Mountain Air Publishing Company, Orem, Utah, 1979.

Twitchell, Paul, *Herbs, The Magic Healers.* Illuminated Way Press, Menlo Park California, 1971.

Wade, Carlson, *Bee Pollen and Your Health.* Keats Publishing, Inc., New Caanan, Connecticutt, 1978.

Walker, Norman W.D.Sc.Ph.D. *Colon Health, the Key to A Vibrant Life.* O'Sullivan Woodside and Company, Phoenix, Arizona, 1979.

Whitehouse, Geoffrey T.F.R.S.H., M.N.I.M.H. *Every Woman's Guide To Natural Health.* Thorsons Publishers Limited, Wellingborough, Northamptonshire, 1974.

Index

Glaucoma, 62
Gout, 96, 97

H

Habit, 30
Hair, 28, 54, 55, 56
Hangovers, 132
Headaches, 29, 48, 49, 50
Healing Crisis, 30
Heart, 8, 17, 105, 106, 110, 127, 137
Heartburn, 17
Hemorrhage, 74
Hemorrhoids, 115, 116
Herbal Shampoo, 55, 88
Herpes, 57
Honey, 45, 139
Hormone Balancers, 23, 26, 28, 73-76, 79, 82, 118
Hot Bath, 43, 44
Hot Flashes, 73
Hydrochloric Acid, 5, 6, 17
Hyperactive Children, 52
Hypoglycemia, 103

Herbs,
Aloe Vera, 6, 12, 34, 35, 47, 55, 58, 60, 61, 75, 87, 92, 102, 104, 115, 122, 131
Anise, 53, 91, 109, 112
Alfalfa, 10, 20, 23, 26, 48, 49, 52, 55, 78, 82, 85, 87, 92, 94, 96, 106, 109, 112, 134, 136, 137, 138, 140
Angelica Root, 24, 25, 27, 75, 101
Apple Pectin, 106
Barberry Rootbark, 9, 11, 20, 23-25, 27, 28, 52, 75, 76, 95, 101, 109, 117, 121, 130, 131
Bayberry, 27, 28, 43, 45, 50, 63, 64, 66, 76, 93, 134
Bee Pollen, 20, 26, 27, 28, 94, 117, 134
Birch Leaves, 24, 25, 75, 101
Bistort, 104
Black Cohosh, 23, 25, 26, 27, 35, 48, 61, 66, 73, 74, 76, 79, 80, 82, 86, 93, 95, 96, 97, 99, 107, 109, 112, 117, 118, 119, 129, 136
Black Walnut, 15, 28, 31, 53, 54, 56, 57, 60, 64, 74, 75, 76, 91, 97, 107, 109, 112, 114, 117, 121, 126, 127, 130, 134, 140

Herbs (continued)

Blessed Thistle, 23-26, 28, 66, 73, 74, 75, 76, 79, 82, 89, 93, 97, 101, 118
Blue Cohosh, 86, 108
Brigham Tea (Desert Tea), 53, 61, 91, 93, 94, 97, 109, 112, 136
Bromelian, 96
Buckthorn, 9-11, 20, 23, 25, 27, 52, 95, 109, 121, 130
Buchu Leaves, 104
Bugleweed Herb, 15
Burdock, 11, 24, 25, 27, 52, 58, 93, 94, 95, 96, 97, 109, 121, 130

Capsicum (Cayenne Pepper), 9, 10, 15, 20, 23-28, 35, 42-46, 48, 50, 53, 61, 63, 64, 66, 70, 72-74, 76, 79, 82, 84, 91, 93, 94, 96, 97, 99, 103, 104, 108-118, 120, 126, 127, 129, 131, 134, 136, 139
Cascara Sagrada, 4, 9-12, 16, 20, 23-25, 27, 52, 95, 101, 109, 117, 121, 130
Catnip, 17, 18, 27, 33, 48, 49, 52, 75, 76, 87, 101, 117, 121, 130
Centaury Herb, 96
Chamomile, 24, 25, 43, 45, 48, 52, 75, 87, 89, 99, 101, 126, 130
Chaparrel, 11, 15, 24, 25, 27, 52, 54, 93, 94, 95, 96, 97, 109, 120, 121, 130, 136
Chickweed, 61, 62, 70, 72, 73, 76, 77, 84, 93, 94, 117, 121, 127, 129, 130, 136
Chlorophyll, 11, 12, 20, 34, 75, 81, 93, 102, 103
Cinnamon, 103
Clove Flower, 43, 45, 50
Comfrey, 6, 9, 16, 20, 27, 28, 42, 43, 48, 49, 54-56, 60, 76-78, 82, 85, 87, 92, 94, 96, 104, 106, 109, 112, 117, 121, 129-131, 134, 136, 137, 140

Couch Grass, 9, 20, 23, 25, 131
Cramp Bark, 27, 28, 73, 75, 82, 101, 118
Culver's Root, 9, 16, 27, 117, 121, 131
Cyani Herb, 76, 117, 121, 130

Damiana, 70, 72, 73, 84, 85

ABOUT THE AUTHOR

Venus and her daughter, Summer, live in Ramona, California. They have a cozy little house surrounded by 14, oat-strewn acres.

They like to sit on their flower-decked front porch and watch their peacock friends swing on the gate.

When not sunning and watching swinging fowl, Venus is working on two more books, due out whenever.

She has a B.A. in commercial art, a teaching credential, a background in home businesses and mail order, studied at Dominion Herbal College of Canada and trained under Drs. John R. Christopher, Bernard Jensen and assorted others. She has lectured on herbs, multi-level marketing and home businesses throughout the United States and Canada. She has also worked as an Herbalist, Iridologist and herb store owner for five years.

RANSOM HILL PRESS PUBLICATIONS

___The Outrageous Herb Lady .... 12.95_____
Venus Andrecht

___The Herb Lady's Notebook .... 12.95_____
Venus Andrecht

___MLM Magic .... 14.95_____
Venus andrecht

___Poems That Tell Me Who I Am ....4.95_____
Margaret McWhorter

___Autumn Leaves (poetry).....................................4.95_____
Margaret McWhorter

___Tea Cup Tales..7.95_____
(*How to read tea leaves*)
Margaret McWhorter

___San Diego County
WRITERS & PUBLISHERS RESOURCE GUIDE .... 19.95 ____
Margaret L. McWhorter

___Drift on the River ....9.95_____
Tales of a Modern Day Thoreau
Harold Rozelle

___Whisperings of My Soul ....3.00_____
Henry Kotschorek

California Residents add 8% **tax**   Sub-Total_____

Shipping: $2.00 for first book   Tax_____

$.50 for each addditonal book   Shipping_____

Make checks payable to:
Ransom Hill Press   Total_____
P.O. Box 325
Ramona, CA 92065

Name _____

Address _____

City_____ State____ Zip_____

Prices subject to change without notice